McGraw Hill

8/12/74

Standing order

CONCILIUM
Religion in the Seventies

CONCILIUM

New Series: Volume 4, Number 10: Pastoral Theology

THE EXPERIENCE OF DYING

Edited by
Norbert Greinacher and Alois Müller

Herder and Herder

1974
HERDER AND HERDER NEW YORK
815 Second Avenue
New York 10017

ISBN: 0-8164-2578-7

Library of Congress Catalog Card Number: 73-17905

Printed in the United States

CONTENTS

Editorial

DEATH can be treated as the Church's ultimate weapon: "You'll see, when he's on his death-bed he'll be glad enough to see the priest."

Reaction against this misuse of a basic human situation and this misunderstanding of the Christian hope of salvation should not lead us to forget that death is really an important and unavoidable point of entry for the religious question and the question of transcendence. Since for human beings existence is a conscious experience, they are able to ask about its meaning. Of the many meanings which are recognized or offered, some are of their nature limited. The meaning of a course of medical treatment, for example, is the restoration of health. Other meanings are not limited by nature and indeed we feel that their disappearance is a contradiction of their meaning. The most abrupt disappearance of many meanings is, of course, death. This assertion is only fully valid when the anthropological dimension of our question contains the category of meaning as well as the category of person. What death questions is not the meaning of various effects on our contemporaries or descendants, but the meaning of personal existence as such.

Since transcendence is the negation of limitations of meaning, and in the case of death is confronted with a time barrier and a subject barrier, it must negate these. It must show that the absolute barrier of time is not a barrier for it, that the potentially transcendent subject does not cease to exist as a result of

7

death any more than transcendent meaning. This is not the answer to the religious question; it is the question itself.

Everyone agrees that death is an urgent matter for human beings, however they react to it. If we let ourselves be impressed by this fact, rather than constructing an anthropology of our own in which things would be different, we may regard death, at least provisionally, as being what it always has been, the highest peak of man's question about the meaning of human life and the embodiment of the question of transcendence.

The community of those who believe in Jesus as the one who has overcome death has clearly to face the challenge of death. It has no need to apologize for the fact that death has always been close to the heart of Christianity. The interest of the Church and theology in death has a very wide range, and includes the anthropological issue of mortality, the question of "life after death" and its soteriological categories (eternal salvation or rejection), the "liturgy of the dead", "death in preaching", and so on. Any of these divisions would easily justify an issue of *Concilium* to itself. We have chosen a limited area, not the least important—that of man at the moment of death. This involves a particular practical and theological task, that of bringing Christians to a full human and religious understanding of death which will enable them to face their own deaths with an adequate understanding and to perform for others in their deaths the services common humanity demands. It also gives the community the responsibility of supporting its members at the end in the same way as it did in life, and also of contributing a critical and humane attitude to the phenomenon of death in society.

Christians who talk about death are in danger of knowing all the answers. Death has been part of the experience of mankind for millennia, but of the Christian experience of death for only two thousand years. Even today all men undergo the experience of death and only a fraction of them are Christians. For this reason *Concilium*'s first aim has been to provide the facts about how people die, what they think and say about death and what they know about death. What is worth criticizing is worth discussing and we must take other people's views (Marx's for example) seriously. The Christian understanding of reality cannot be served by limiting our perception of reality. Above all, we must know how contemporary man reacts to death. Only then will we know what our faith enables us to say to him.

After all, faith must enable us to say something to him. There are so many approaches—the biblical message and lived faith (spirituality),[1] our duty to our fellow men, our social duty and our prophetic role in society, and the Church's own life in the encounter with death.

The age-old general human view, that death was everyone's unavoidable destiny, has been abandoned. There are people today who have the measure of transcendence. For them, life after death will be earthly life, and death will be a disease that we will conquer and abolish like tuberculosis or polio. Christians do not need to console themselves with the thought that this is just the fad of a few rich (or efficient) eccentrics who will soon look rather silly. If attempts like these succeeded, they would simply make the question of transcendence all the more urgent. Besides, Christians already have reasons enough of their own for regarding death as part of human life and for giving the message of Jesus as the one who has overcome death practical application in men's deaths no more and no less than in their lives.

NORBERT GREINACHER
ALOIS MÜLLER

[1] We regret that an important article on the Christian spirituality of death could not be written in time owing to the illness of the author.

PART I
ARTICLES

Johann Hofmeier

The Present-Day Experience
of Death

I. The Problem

ATTITUDES to death and dying in Western society have changed
within the space of a century. There are many signs of this.
There are people trying with complete seriousness to outwit
death by the use of refrigeration techniques. Social critics talk
about a new form of existence in a world in which a total
transformation would lead to the abolition of death. Others de-
plore the way people are forced to die in public institutions.
They condemn the way in which the dying are banished from
society and death is made taboo or a merely private or even a
commercial affair, since this results in those faced with death
feeling uncertain and helpless. Historians of ideas have isolated
an intellectual change. Until well on in the nineteenth century,
they say, the Christian faith dominated Western thinking,
formed people's world-view and influenced their experience of
death. This influence is fast disappearing.

A change in attitudes to death and dying means a change in
people's understanding of themselves and of the purpose of life.
They are forced to ask if their new attitude is the right one.
The question is also brought into prominence by the conflict
of two opposing views, the one which says that death is being
repressed, and the one which speaks of a change in attitudes as
a result of a change in the social structure and age structure of
society.

The remarks that follow are in no sense an answer to these

questions. They will do no more than describe present-day man's experience of death and indicate its sources and presuppositions. "Experience" here will be taken to mean the preception acquired from continual dealings with people and things. Present-day man's subjective experience of death and the social factors which influence that experience are interrelated. In his experience of death the individual is influenced by collective ideas and standardized behaviour patterns. In the Western world there are three main areas in which changes have taken place which affect our present-day experience of death: medicine, social conventions and violent death and its representations.

II. MEDICINE AND THE MODERN EXPERIENCE OF DEATH

In the past century, advances in knowledge and technique have changed medicine and this has brought about a change in the experience of dying. There are three main aspects of this. Life expectancy has increased. The care of health has become highly specialized and been divided into many branches. There are now more ways of influencing the process of death from outside.

Higher life expectancy is the result of medical advances. Since the beginning of the nineteenth century the relation between death-rate and birth-rate has been continually changing in favour of the birth-rate. Medicine succeeded in checking the mortality rate among infants, children and mothers in childbirth and in pushing back the frontier of death by means of medical techniques ranging from standard health procedures to organ transplantation and resuscitation. In the Roman Empire, average life expectancy was roughly twenty years, in Germany in 1875 thirty-five years, but by 1950 it had risen to sixty-five years. As a result, the frequency of death per 10,000 of the population has fallen in the last 150 years from around 25–30 to 10–12 cases a year. The effect of this increased life expectancy on man's experience of death has been that direct contact with death and dying has become rarer. Whereas previously everyone inevitably came in contact with death in early childhood and had seen the dead body of some relative, this is now true of only a very small percentage of children. The result of this is "that death has disappeared as an object of primary socialization, particularly when one realizes that the generation gap amounts today to little more than twenty years and that children escape from the socializing influence of their directional family at the age of fifteen at the latest. It is this early phase of socialization, however, which is crucial for the basic grasp and interpretation of reality, and in particular for the way a person processes it emotionally."[1]

As well as reducing the frequency of direct contact with death, medical progress has also weakened the intensity of the experience of death. This results partly from the structure of health care. Medical technology has led inevitably to the existence of many different institutions with specialized, functional services. Illness and death now occur within a different frame of reference. Events which even a few years ago took place in the family have now been transferred to the appropriate specialized field. In this field all those involved are expected to adopt the appropriate roles. The dying person is a patient among many other patients, no longer the dying father or dying neighbour. The doctor and nursing staff are professionals who are expected to provide the necessary services and to be able to maintain life. Every death places them in a conflict of roles. This conflict makes them insecure, and they retreat to their purely professional functions and skills, thereby losing more and more of their confidence and their ability to make contact with the dying.

Relatives too are forced into specific roles in a hospital. They are visitors, tolerated only at fixed times. Emotional ties are of course prominent during visits, but they can only be expressed in ways appropriate to the situation. It is normally impossible for friends and relatives to undertake the care of the patient in hospital or to follow the course of the disease and death. This shift of roles means a loss in both quantitative contact with death and qualitative experience of death, because the experience of death is less intensive. This does not prevent the death

---

[1] Alois Hahn, *Einstellung zum Tod und ihre soziale Bedingtheit* (Stuttgart, 1968), p. 23. In West Germany in 1971 the death rate was 11.8 per 1000. In Sweden in 1800 it was 25 per 1000, by 1900 it had fallen to 16 and by 1945 to 10. On average today it takes ten to fifteen years before a member of a family dies. This means that in our time a person must be fifty before he experiences the same number of deaths as a twenty-year-old in 1820 (Hahn, 13–22).

of a loved one from being a painful experience, but it prevents many people from being affected by the death of another person in a way that makes them aware of their own mortality.

Medical progress has a third aspect. This has to do with the formation of the collective consciousness, which takes place at pre-conscious levels. Scientific medicine seeks to understand and use the laws of life and death. This means that in present-day man's spontaneous attitudes life and death become more and more things which can be controlled, as other areas of nature have before them. From an historical point of view this means that man has succeeded in removing something of the mystery from yet another area of reality. Issues such as birth control and family planning, rejuvenation, prolongation of life and euthanasia in the widest sense should be seen against the background of the ability to control the laws of life and death.

Of course, death confronts medical skill with insuperable obstacles. Nevertheless doctors have succeeded not only in postponing the point of death for many people, but also in changing the process of death itself. It is now only in exceptional cases that death is painful. The word "agony" is hardly appropriate now, since drugs make it increasingly possible to drift into a peaceful sleep. Such advances encourage the illusion of one's own immortality, which psychoanalysts say everyone is convinced of in their unconscious. This illusion acquires all the more force in a period when changed social structures have reduced the frequency and intensity of contact with death. It is rooted in the urge to live which thrusts towards the maintenance and extension of life, and is able to prevail in spite of the facts principally because reduced contact with death means fewer possibilities for control by reality.

III. THE PRESENT-DAY EXPERIENCE OF DEATH IN THE FIELD OF SOCIAL CONVENTIONS

Medicine is embedded in social conventions. It is determined by conventions, and itself shapes conventions. For this reason dying and death affect not only the individual but also society. Death always requires the proper public reactions. These have to do with three basic factors—dealing with the body (paying respects to the body, the announcement of death, grave, burial and cemetery); social and economc security, the reduction of the effects of death (inheritance laws, insurance, role substitution); mourning.

The funeral trade has brought about a marked change in dealings with the body. Services which were previously performed by relatives and friends are now undertaken by professonal funeral specialists. They reify the treatment of the body and spare relatives the emotional confrontation. This corresponds to the functional structure of society, and caters for uncertainty in dealing with the dead. Both economic interests and the needs of the bereaved are met if the undertakers take over more and more of the tasks which arise in connection with death, the public announcement of death through advertisements or notices, arrangements for paying respects to the body, the funeral and wake (if any). For the present-day experience of death, this means that fewer and fewer people have anything to do with the funeral process and people less and less frequently have occasion to face the reality of death. Relatives and friends withdraw from contact with the dead person and adopt the public role of bereavement.

Of much more public importance than the details of the funeral are the socio-economic arrangements in case of death. Laws of inheritance, wills and a great variety of types of insurance regulate property relations and relieve the individual. This brings about an unconscious change in attitudes to death because the death of a relative no longer threatens one's own existence in the same way as in the past and there is no longer a need to fear the heavy material consequences of one's own death on surviving relatives. The group, too, does not experience such a total break in its internal relations.

In the feudal agricultural societies and bourgeois cities of the past, mutual relations among people were more extensive and formed more of a system. The circle of "relatives" in this wider sense was comparatively closed, and the relations themselves had an affective character, and were not limited to economic functions. Within the group the dead person was irreplaceable because the relations were attached to him personally. The loss could only be made good by a restructuring of the group in which new affective ties had to be formed. On the other hand, in a functional society the loss of a group member can be made good by means of a substitute and as soon as someone is found activities resume their normal course. The loss of a group member may be the result, not merely of death, but also of a change of job, the reaching of retirement age or prolonged illness. This means that death as such is not necessarily an occasion for mourning. This is connected with the fact that a person's ties with workmates, friends, leisure companions and family no longer involve all his roles. The dead person may also quite often not have lived with his family, but in his own home, and maybe even in a different town.

The funeral profession, social support and economic replacement influence mourning customs, but even more the action of mourning, which has the psychological and social function of absorbing the loss of the dead person. The action of mourning now retains a public character merely in the announcement of death and the funeral, which indicates who this person was, husband, father, friend, neighbour, colleague, superior, subordinate or partner.[2] Mourning customs which go beyond an announcement at the time of the funeral are becoming less and less intelligible in a city culture because people who had merely functional and not emotional relations with the dead person feel no need of actual mourning. In a functional society, signs of mourning, with their emotional charge, may disturb the orderly course of life and work. The only exception consists of the very few people who had emotional ties with the dead person at the time of death and for whom he or she cannot be replaced. It is these people who feel most keenly that they must remain alone with their grief because displaying it in public will have an alienating effect. An example of this is that mourning clothes are increasingly losing their meaning. Society no longer knows how to treat a mourner. This prompts the hypothesis that present-day, and still more future, dealings with death will start less and less from external contact with death or contact

[2] Christian von Ferber, "Der Tod. Ein unbewältigtes Problem für Mediziner und Soziologen', *Kölner Zeitschrift für Soziologie und Sozialpsychologie* 22 (1970), p. 239.

with social reactions to death. Instead private feelings will be much more important in our experience of death.

Death is the final breaking of ties to possessions and associates. In itself it has no meaning since it means the end of any possibility of further relationships. Many preliminary stages of this final separation occur in life, which develops as a constant process of binding and loosing, giving and taking. An anticipation of the final separation can be experienced in every process of separation. Jean Améry, in his essay "On Ageing", talks about experiences which lie along the line of this constant separation, experiences which inevitably increase with age because withdrawal from social ties becomes increasingly marked.[3] Améry describes experiences which can be described as experiences of a death which grows from within, becomes more and more prominent and is felt as a negation of life. Experience of this death increases during life, just as experiences of separation increase through life. These inner experiences of death also help, as much as external contact with death, to form people's attitudes to death. These attitudes vary from person to person with age, particular experiences, life history and character, but follow a common pattern because all men are exposed to the same external stimuli. When this inner experience of death forces a person to react to it, it may become easier for him to acquire a healthy attitude to death and dying. On the other hand, against this positive assessment we must set another aspect of reality. This is violent death and representations of death in all its gradations.

IV. Present-Day Experience of Death from Violent Death and Representations of Death

Scientific progress and the functional organization of social life reduce the burden on the individual and make it possible for him to have an attitude to death which is not dominated by fear, uncertainty and worry, but by a realistic awareness of the limits of his life. There are, however, contradictions which qualify this optimistic view, in that the same society permits

[3] Jean Améry, Über das Altern. Revolution und Resignation (Stuttgart, 1968).

various forms of violent biological and social death, death in accidents, war and by execution, and the denial of participation in social life to the old, the sick, the handicapped, those marked out for punishment and those suffering from mental strain. Some of these make explicit by suicide what society has already done to them.[4] Objectively, violent death, particularly in war, increases the frequency of direct contact with death, but, in an amazingly large number of cases, fails to produce profound experiences or shock. The appalling death-toll of the last wars seems to have had relatively few effects in the Western world and made little difference to attitudes to death, either because in order to maintain life it was necessary to get away as quickly as possible from the mass deaths and trivialize them, or because violent killing sanctioned by society does not shock people. General feeling respects the soldier who kills in war provided he keeps to the recognized rules, and praises him as a hero when he is killed himself.[5]

Self-preservation justifies the violent killing of other men in war and the demand that the individual should sacrifice his life for the group. But self-preservation is also the source of the arguments for society's use of the threat of death and of execution. The threat of death is used in society as a means of social control, to prevent deviations from social norms.[6] Life imprisonment has the same social function because the condemned person

[4] Cf. Gregor Siefert, "Der Tod, die sicherste Prognose. Anmerkungen zu einer Soziologie des Todes', *Diakonia* 3 (1972), pp. 328-33. Statistics perhaps support the view that high accident rates may bring about a change in the experience of death, in that it will increase the number of those who have direct contact with death in early life. According to a publication of the Bavarian statistical office for May 1972, 3,581 people were killed in road accidents in Bavaria in 1971, and a further 136 died within a month from the effects of accidents. This is about 40 road deaths per 100,000 of the total population. Accidents of all kinds in Bavaria killed 7,418. Also interesting in this connection is a comparison of road accident figures for the *Land* Nordrhein-Westfalen for the period 1962-1966. In contrast to the general development, the proportion of young men increased in accidents involving failure to control a vehicle or running undue risks.

[5] Arnold Toynbee, "Changing Attitudes towards Death in the Modern Western World", in *Man's Concern with Death* (London, 1968), pp. 122-32.

[6] Werner Fuchs, *Todesbilder in der modernen Gesellschaft* (Frankfurt, 1970), p. 202.

is cut off from communication and is dead to society. Societies require the deaths of their members to preserve particular goods of life; they glorify this voluntary abandonment of life and accept violent death for the preservation of the goods of life as unavoidable. It cannot be denied that, except in so far as this serves the development of life, individual and social benefit are here in conflict. This is the only explanation of the fact that in the decades of industrialization, the development of technology and urbanization Western societies completely refused to sacrifice economic, technical and scientific progress to more human working conditions (the prevention of damage to life and health from the work process).

The tendencies to self-preservation, individual development and especially individual enjoyment require a socially sanctioned attitude to violent death. Individual and social psychological mechanisms have an effect here, since everyone is involved in some way in a violent death, either as the victim or an anonymous member of the society which in the last resort sanctions violent death. The victim may be a despised enemy, a person who has committed a crime or been convicted, but he may also be a careless or carefree young person in a traffic accident. Alternatively the victim may be a hero, a hero of labour or of his profession, a hero in the performance of his duties. In this case he is accorded unlimited respect, and the anonymous member of society identifies with him. In every case a barrier is erected between the person who is violently killed and the person who is unaffected which prevents the experience of death. Only in exceptional cases does violent death lead to an experience of death; this is in cases where a person's acquired identity enables him to separate himself from his own society and, in violent situations, even protest against it.

Sigmund Freud put forward a remarkable but plausible explanation for the fact that a person can be an anonymous member of a society which itself produces death by violence and does not condemn, but honours killing in the service of society and demands the sacrifice of life. Freud talks of a murderous instinct which exists in the deepest layers of the personality. In war a regression to these layers takes place.[7] In everyday life this unconscious tendency makes itself visible in the need to remove unpleasant obstacles, whether things or persons. This unconscious tendency may explain why direct and indirect forms of violence and their effects are so little noticed and do not produce an experience of death in present-day man.

If this is true, and the various forms of violent death do not result in an experience of death for modern man, or only do so in exceptional cases, one might nevertheless think that the mass media, and in particular representations of death, would encourage such experiences. In Western society we are extensively informed. Newspapers, radio and illustrated magazines bring us reports of disaster and death from all parts of the world. Images of violence occupy a large proportion of time in films and on television. We might expect that modern man might be emotionally affected by this frequent indirect contact with death. However, all the indications are that press reports have only a superficial effect and that filmed reports frequently have the opposite effect. Film reports seem to deaden rather than awaken feeling for underlying content.

In addition, pictures of violence also seem to have another effect. They strengthen a person's existing illusion of his own immortality and thereby counteract any experience of death. There are quite standard patterns for films, in which the figure with whom the audience can identify is successful, confident and immune from death.

In conclusion, the various forms of violent and dramatized death may be said to give the individual illusory relief. This works in the opposite direction from the relief given by medical progress and functionalization in society and is an obstacle to a rational confrontation with death. Such a rational approach is less influenced by fear of death and worry about suffering or the needs of survivors, whereas the illusion reinforces the tendencies which go with the repression of death. It also prevents the relief which could result from progress in the medical and social spheres from taking effect, and prevents any consideration of

[7] Sigmund Freud, "Thoughts for the Times on War and Death", Standard Edition, Vol. XIV, pp. 275–300.

the nature of a meaningful and responsible life, since this is connected with the problem of the proper attitude to death. This, however, brings us to the limits of an analysis of present-day experience of death which is based mainly on external realities and does not go into philosophical and theological implications.

Translated by Francis McDonagh

Karl Bloching

The Reflection of Death in Contemporary Literature

MODERN literature reflects our experience of death and our attitudes to it. The picture shows a broad spectrum. Literature reproduces all the various attitudes and reactions provoked by this phenomenon. Death has been a literary theme from the earliest times, but man's view of the theme has changed. Frameworks such as religion and myth which previously determined or supported attitudes have been questioned, have become unclear or have disappeared. It is the function of literature to uncover these frameworks and give them substance, to examine them and reproduce them in particular forms. It is generally agreed that man is characterized by the need to face the inevitability of death. He is the creature who can die consciously.

I

Rilke saw man as constantly involved in the polarity of death and birth. "Inside us day by day are birth and death." One's own death and the fact of death appear as superior beings with power over man, always in and around man. Rilke found in abstract death a possibility of concealment because it is always present. His view, which provided a comforting answer for many people in the days of the great Rilke cult, has not, however, been reflected in the work of other writers, some of whom have believed that the inevitability of death makes the whole of life ridiculous.

II

Not very long ago, one of these writers, the Frenchman Henri de Montherlant, took his own life at the age of seventy-seven. Adventure and reflection about life, death and women were the motive forces of his life. A sentence from his diary runs: "Women and death call to us—and say nothing." Montherlant regarded everything as doomed to die, but did not draw the conclusion that man had to be resigned. Instead, he tried to squeeze the maximum pleasure out of life. When he was no longer capable of this and the fragility of age and illness was making life a burden to him, he chose the moment of his own death. He thought it right to stop his life-clock himself and to throw away what now appeared to him as the refuse of his self.

The Austrian Thomas Bernhard's work is a continuing variation on the theme that subjection to the law of death makes everything unbearable. For him, death makes everything ridiculous and replaceable. His analyses and stories develop a gloomy exploration of this destiny of man without a trace of joy or hope. Key words and concepts in his works are error, hopelessness, monotony, decline, chaos, emptiness, madness, failure, loneliness, pain and paradox. It is a powerful *De profundis*, a phenomenology of gloomy dedication to death, excluding all rational, technocratic or optimistic world views. For him, since life is death by instalments, there can be no meaningful structures and no certainty, even in the short term. Everything falls away into a constant process of death.

III

Other writers have an attitude of stoic, heroic protest. Ernest Hemingway often depicted men on the frontier of death and about to take their leave. Through these figures, he probed into Western ideals and attitudes and put them to the test, only to find that they in fact contain nothing. Hemingway was full of a deep melancholy, a sense that love, courage and mythical action parables (such as bullfighting) cannot take away the objectivity of death. It is possible to rise above this distress for moments, but then one falls back. It is his fate that he must some time sink into cold nature, into an icy nothingness. Hemingway constructed his figures in such a way that they could exist with dignity and composure. They do not fall apart (as far as the reader can see), but end proudly. In my view, this attitude conceals the fact that they simply merge into something inevitable. In addition, such an attitude requires that a person must have armed himself, and excludes consideration of other attitudes or questioning of one's own attitude.

For Albert Camus the inevitability of death is one of the most impressive features of an absurd existence. Far from making life worthless, it does the opposite. This absurd life becomes an absolute. For Camus speculation on existence beyond time is a betrayal of existence. Man's attention must be concentrated on his life and on giving a human form to existence and social life. In Camus's novel *The Plague*, Dr Rieux's guiding principle is "One must be satisfied with people and with one's miserable, magnificent love." This doctor, one of the finest figures of atheistic heroism, contemplates death around him. In the city in which the plague, the incalculable bacillus of death, is loose, he sees that people betray what in health they hold most sacred, family, loyalty, ties of blood and friendship. Dr Rieux does not however, despair. He is not depressed by the fact that his fellow men are like this, but he accepts it. It is man's nature, and it is good. Death is the terrible end. One cannot prepare for the inevitable end of life, only accept it.

IV

In recent years a number of books have appeared in which writers have described their own experience of death.

Anne Philippe, in her book *The Space of a Sigh*, describes her experience of the death of her husband, the famous French actor Gérard Philippe. She knew about his fatal illness, but was not allowed to tell him anything about it. Keeping it a secret was irreconcilable with the honesty which husband and wife otherwise practised. The dishonesty tormented her just as much as the fear of losing her treasured husband. She managed not to let anything show. She did not think about his death and about losing him until he was dead.

His sudden death brought her to the edge of despair. She

bore it in the same attitude of surrender that Camus described and preached in his writings. She interpreted the mystery of death in the framework of a mythical cosmic unity. She felt herself a part of a cosmic law which was beyond rational understanding and incapable of more precise definition than that it was the source from which man came and to which he returned in death. She had experienced this unity with the cosmos in her harmonious and happy marriage. Her hymn to the happiness of her love merges into praise of happy absorption into the cosmos. She makes the perfection and beauty of her happiness the basis of a belief in a mysterous world unity concealed in happiness. Since life and love were all that mattered to her, while her husband was alive she did not think of death. The fact that someone had to die left her heartbroken. Death showed her the terrible side of reality. Death destroys everything, but she transcended it through the mythical fiction of the universe's gentle embrace.

In *A Very Easy Death,* Simone de Beauvoir described the death of her mother. The author was so shaken by fear, revulsion and protest, that she almost suffered physical and mental breakdown. Her mother's life had been dominated by subservience, religious faith, sacrifice and an adherence to bourgeois conventions which her daughter had completely rejected, but the old woman's pain and will to live showed her daughter the power of old age, the strength of the body and of death.

In the book, the daughter contemplates her mother. The old woman is helpless and fragile. She is in severe pain. The daughter looks after her mother. She watches over her and helps her. She protects her from unwanted visitors and does everything she can to keep the old woman from realizing her true situation. She lets her mother believe the illness can be cured and that she will get better. Simone de Beauvoir finds this dishonest, but she is keenly aware how brutal it would be to suddenly reveal to the old woman her real situation. Nor does this fit with Simone de Beauvoir's existentialist attitude. She does not know what to say to comfort her mother.

Simone de Beauvoir (and the reader) are forced to become aware of what it means to face a terrible and painful end. For the author it means sinking into nothingness. The mother is a practising Catholic, but the daughter cannot understand why with the approach of death her mother does not look for comfort in the sacraments and religion. The old woman doesn't pray, but busies herself with pointless everyday details of life, or does crossword puzzles. The reader may wonder whether the old woman was not deceived by the trivial nature of the consolation that surrounded her.

Christa Wolf's book *Nachdenken über Christa T.* ("Thoughts about Christa T.") is a thoughtful review of the life and death of her friend, Christa T. The reader is introduced to the sympathetic figure of a sensitive, romantically melancholic young woman. Christa T. was an idealist. She was a teacher, and believed in the promises of the socialist paradise. She believed in the perfect utopia. Gradually she began to have doubts. She refused to make concessions. She married and had a happy marriage and children. Then, quite suddenly, she became ill with leukemia and died. For her friend it was inconceivable.

Christa Wolf shares with the reader her confusion and search for an answer. The process of death becomes a problem in this book as it did for Simone de Beauvoir. The longing for beauty, perfection and paradise which the author's friend searched for but could not find in the socialist system become questions for the reader. Death is lonely. It is surrounded by deceptive consolations. The dying person is not given a chance to find advice or explanation in her situation. She is a stranger among the living. They cannot help her because they are not prepared for death and have not decided what they think about it. This makes the situation of death something terrible and strange. Death becomes a crisis for the survivors, and yet it is doubtful whether things will be any different for them in this situation, or whether they too will not be left in a situation of blindness and loneliness.

Willi Kramp's *Der letzte Feind* ("The Last Enemy") is a report of the death of his brother. The motto of Kramp's book is a sentence from the Bible: "The last enemy to be destroyed is death." Kramp is a Christian, and he describes the death of his brother, a Protestant pastor. The brother knows that he has cancer and is going to die. From time to time the hope flickers that, after all, he will recover. But the end is too certain. The death is described without any attempt to dress it up, without any pseudo-religious or ideological ornament. The incurable disease destroys the life of this man amid agonizing pain. Sedatives can no longer suppress the pain. The agonizing death is accepted in faith, but there remains the puzzle of the senseless torment of the pain. The dying man comes through this torture and accepts death. Here, in faith, the last enemy, death, is defeated.

Marie-Luise Kaschnitz has written poems describing the horror of death in war. In her diary, *Wohin denn ich?*, the author describes a period of about six months in her own life. Her husband has died and this death has affected her so deeply that she too is near death. The death that threatens her is not a physical one. She slips into a state of mental numbness, an in-between state of psychic evaporation. Slowly, aroused by external circumstances, she finds her way back to everyday life and to writing. The only way she can get her life back, however, is by recognizing her loved husband as a continually existing person, with whom communication is possible. The dead man becomes a living person for her against the background of her Christian faith. The recovery of her life and contact with others goes hand in hand with thinking about God and recovery of belief and a relationship to the Church.

V

In his *Tagebuch 1946–1949*, Max Frisch wrote: "The consciousness of our mortality is a precious gift, not just the mortality, which we share with newts, but our consciousness of it. It is only this that makes our existence human, makes it an adventure and preserves us from the perfect boredom of the gods."

In the diary-novel *Homo Faber*, Frisch portrays an engineer, Faber, who has tried to eliminate from his life everything that cannot be expressed in mathematical terms and to shape his life on the principle, "No mysticism; mathematics is enough." He gets bogged down in guilt and becomes uncertain, but tries by every means to maintain the fiction that life can be mastered by calculation and reason. He meets his old fiancée, Hanna. She confronts his outlook with her experience of life. She says that as a scientist, and in his particular case as a pure scientist, who would allow validity to no other approach or sensibility than those of science and mathematics, he has tried to arrange the world in such a way that he does not need to experience it as opposition. Science, she says, is a trick for doing away with the world as opposition—rarefying it by speed, for instance. Hanna thinks that the fundamental error of the scientist is to attempt to live without thinking of death. She says to Faber: "You treat life not as a form, but as simple addition; it has no relation to time because it has no relation to death." At first Faber cannot understand Hanna's formula for life, "Life is form in time." For him, as a mathematician and scientist, each year of his life is merely the sum of the units of time that can be measured with a clock. Hanna measures life by her suffering and by its distance from death. Life means growing old, approaching death. Hanna realizes too that growing old means that no moment repeats itself and that each must be given its value before the next and before death. Faber does not see his mistake until he is seriously ill and facing the fact that he will not survive an operation or at least not for long. In this situation he begins to be sensitive to the beauty of the world and the value of life as such. He realizes that he is not enough for himself; he opens himself willingly to let another person love him, be attached to him in friendship. He frees himself from his pride and the belief that only what is measurable and mathematically expressible is valid. He longs to be eternal.

In this book dying and death appear as a gift. They open a person's eyes to the personal and aesthetic dimension in life. In the possible and probable situation of death he recognizes finitude and eternity.

In later books and plays, Max Frisch passes a more sceptical judgment on the death situation. The behaviour researcher Kürmann in *Biographie* refuses to make any change in his life to allow for his death. It is clear to the spectator that he refuses to withdraw or change anything because he wants to be proved right. In death, Kürmann clamps himself to his identity and fixes it permanently in that instant. He learns nothing and does not become open.

In his *Tagebuch 1966–1967*, Max Frisch describes ageing as a death situation: "Death which cuts off life at the flood is becoming a rarity—fear of death has shifted to fear of ageing, i.e. of going dotty. ... We control entry into life, and it is time for us to control the exit too" (p. 95). The reader is made to contemplate and think about the possibility of man deciding on his own death. If, as Max Frisch believes, life is the sum of actions which remain accidental, this already raises the question why we should not control death.

VI

The French writer Jean Cayrol describes his work as "Lazarenic". His books describe the "living dead", people in Holy Saturday situations. In 1963, Cayrol published *Le soleil froid*, the story of a traveller. In a breathless monologue he goes through the story of his life and in the end it turns out that he is dying. This active man, driven hectically without a break, is the type of a modern Wandering Jew, who plays tricks on himself with his own meaning. He gives himself a meaning that he does not possess. He uses slick talk to cover up his fear, and above all his fear of an accident. As he lies in the terminal ward of a French country hospital he reviews his own life. In death he clings to his self-deception: "I am immortal. I am the eternal popular travelling salesman and life could not go on without my coming and going. I give life its real movement." At the end, "Hell, I'm dying." What he does not realize, but what the reader perhaps sees, is that changes of work and pastimes, travel, power over others, being a Don Juan, and confidence trickery are only escapes.

VII

Modern literature presents a broad spectrum of attitudes towards death and dying. These works of literature make the phenomenon of death impressively clear, and leave the reader who accepts it with a choice. They do not just convey information or report facts. They show people in a crisis, broken at having to be present helplessly at a death and witness indifference or struggle to find a meaning in the process in which a human being with whom one is involved approaches what can be interpreted either as a falling back into nothing, an unreconciled return into nature or as passage through a dark door in hope.

Literature allows one to see into the structure of a widespread way of dealing with death and its results. People try to trivialize or ignore it, but literature answers with a "but". For others, death is simply the power which overshadows everything and sets a question-mark beside it. Death annihilates everything. A third attitude is that death brings us into a crisis in which we can think again about life and make a reappraisal of it. Death forces us to a more realistic revision of our way of life and lets us see the basic structure of life, for example, to recognize finitude or eternity.

Literature brings death close, probes situations, possibilities and attitudes and shows their value, and looks for what is solid or will give support. It also analyses the unfathomable, the fall into the depths, disappearance or annihilation, whether or not death is free. Literature demonstrates possible end situations, and especially the loneliness of the dying and the escape rituals of the living.

Translated by Francis McDonagh

Christoph Käufer

A Medical View of the Process of Death

IN the past recognition of the occurrence of death was a simple matter for the doctor. Life was regarded as ending with the last heartbeat, and death as having occurred when the heart had stopped beating. In addition to the clinically observable absence of the signs of life such as breathing and circulation, in ascertaining death, the doctor or coroner relied on the "certain signs of death" which appear some hours later (rigor mortis, coldness and pallor) and these were accepted as proof of the occurrence of death.

I. PROCESS OF DEATH, UNDERLYING CONDITION AND CAUSE OF DEATH

The process of death can be set in motion by a variety of causes. Carbon tetrachloride poisoning destroys the liver, serious lung inflammation reduces the area of the respiratory surfaces, producing a harmful strain on the circulation. Kidney failure as a result of chronic inflammation produces internal poisoning because harmful by-products of metabolism can no longer be removed. A variety of possible illnesses finally merges into a single cause of death, cardiac arrest. The connection between the underlying condition and the cause of death is often evident in cases of severe injury, when the resulting blood loss leads to irreparable shock or the blocking of a coronary vessel robs the heart muscle of its blood circulation and with it of its oxygen supply, as in myocardial infarction due to blocking of a coronary artery by thrombosis.

33

Death is generally defined as the disappearance of all signs of life in the organism as a whole, while the failure of individual parts of the body is called "necrosis". The terms, heart failure, respiratory failure and liver failure are usually taken to mean the initial stage of an illness or of damage which leads finally to the death of the organism as a whole. This threat to life beginning in various organ systems was recognized long ago by Bichat, who distinguished between the death of the heart, death of the lungs and death of the brain(1).*

II. Loss of Consciousness

In the course of chronic illnesses, consciousness is often reduced at a quite early stage. Typical of this is the hepatic coma or uraemia in the course of liver or kidney failure. The patient gradually slips into a sleep-like state, from which he can at first be roused by speech or other stimulus. Finally he becomes unconscious, comatose, until after a period of hours or days death occurs.

In other situations, consciousness is maintained complete without any limitation until death. A striking example of this is a severe pulmonary embolism. Here the patient may appear to be completely well when a blood clot blocks the pulmonary artery and produces immediate heart failure as a reflex. In a few cases the surgeon may succeed in removing the clot by opening the heart cavity. The author knows of successful operations of this sort in which the patients could later remember events which could be shown to have occurred after their hearts had ceased to function. Normally, however, unconsciousness occurs immediately after the stopping of the heart.

III. Cardiac Arrest and Resuscitation

Previously the sudden arrest of cardiac activity, followed immediately by loss of consciousness and the collapse of all other organic systems, could be regarded as the occurrence of death, with the confident assumption that the previously mentioned sure signs of death would appear within a short time. A new situation was produced when modern methods of treatment

* Numbers refer to the bibliography at the end of this article.

made it possible to prolong a life which would otherwise have soon become extinct or to overcome a sudden cardiac arrest by expert massage and electrical stimulation, which, in favourable cases, resulted in true resuscitation.

In cases of threatened or actual respiratory failure as a result of severe cerebral injury, poisoning or the inflammation of the respiratory centre in the brain, artificial respiration can be used. Originally this meant an iron lung, but today breathing apparatus is used in which a system of tubes is connected to the lungs and trachea. This enables the organism to be supplied with oxygen and the otherwise imminent collapse of the circulatory system to be averted.

There is a chance of success only when attempts at reanimation are begun immediately the heart stops, since the stopping of circulation means that the body's oxygen supply is no longer being maintained, and this results within a short time in irreparable damage. The tolerance of the various organs to a failure of their oxygen supply as a result of cardiac arrest depends on their degree of differentiation. Under favourable conditions the heart can survive an interruption of circulation for sixty to ninety minutes, the kidneys for two and a half hours, the liver for twenty to thirty minutes, the lungs for thirty to sixty minutes, and the brain for at the most eight to ten minutes (12).

From both clinical experience and experimental results, it appears that after a circulatory stoppage as short as three to four minutes the extinct consciousness does not return. The brain—and in particular the surface of the cerebral cortex—the activity of which is the basis of consciousness, is more sensitive than any other bodily organ to a lack of food and oxygen. After only a short interruption of circulation the brain cells cease to function —which in clinical terms amounts to immediate loss of consciousness—and if the shortage of oxygen continues they die. Unlike all other cells of the body, the neurones of the brain cannot be regenerated. That is, a destroyed cell of the brain cortex cannot be replaced by a newly produced cell, as is possible in any other part of the body. The quota of neurones present at birth is limited. The quota is very generous, and the body can easily survive a slight loss, but it cannot make it good. Once it occurs, breakdown of brain tissue is final.

After cardiac arrest, if breathing and circulation can be restored in time, consciousness returns, an otherwise certain death is averted, and the reanimated patient goes on living with no ill effects. There are innumerable examples of such resuscitation after cardiac arrest after narcosis, heart infarction, injuries, suffocation, respiratory paralysis and other conditions. If this short period in which recovery of the brain cells is possible passes, however, consciousness does not return. In such cases the heart and circulation can be revived, but the resulting situation is one in which the human personality has been lost. The patient's breathing is adequate, pulse and blood pressure are intact, but he does not respond when spoken to and can make no contact with his environment. The physiognomy shows remarkable grimaces; speech is limited to inarticulate sounds in response to painful stimuli. This state is described medically as an apallic syndrome, which implies that the distinctively human cerebral cortex has ceased to function while the brain stem continues to maintain elementary vital functions such as respiration, circulation and temperature control. How far particular parts of the brain stem such as the thalamus are important in the formation of the deep personality and conscious mental reactions is still not clear from medical research, and cannot be discussed here.

This does not exhaust the range of possible damage to the brain as a result of lack of oxygen. An apallic syndrome results when resuscitation is undertaken after a delay of between three to four minutes and a maximum of eight to ten minutes. If the shortage of oxygen lasts longer, an unusual situation appears. The action of the heart can be restored, but the brain shows no signs of any function. The condition differs from the previously mentioned apallic syndrome in that there is deep unconsciousness with no reaction to any pain stimuli. There is no reaction in any cerebral reflexes. The pupils are dilated and show no reaction. Unassisted breathing stops and the body temperature falls. This situation of complete loss of all brain functions is new to medicine, and was only observed after the introduction of reanimation and mechanical breathing techniques (3, 10). The description of this state as "death of the brain" is appropriate, and implies, in addition to the complete loss of function, that

the state can be shown to be irreversible. This will be discussed
below. In clinical terms the observations agree with experimental
data on the time limits for the resuscitation of various organs
after shortage or lack of oxygen (6, 12).

IV. Criteria of Death: Heart and Brain

The most important result of the possibility of cardiac resuscitation is that cardiac arrest is no longer definitive and cannot
be regarded as a criterion for determining the occurrence of
death. This has produced a vigorous discussion about whether
instead of the heart the brain should be the parameter on whose
functions or lack of function a determination of death should
be based. This is not a sudden anxiety to distinguish between
two categories of death. Since the death of the brain as an
organ very soon brings with it the death of all other organs of
the organism, the determination of death could in principle be
based on the brain. This approach is usually superfluous because
it requires complicated instruments and because the death of
the brain follows within minutes of cardiac arrest (14).

There are, however, a number of practical problems which
make the question relevant. The increasing number of attempts
at resuscitation has produced a depressing situation in medicine.
While in many cases reanimation is unsuccessful and the patient
dies in spite of all efforts, or in others the patient revives and
recovers, many attempts at reanimation result in apallic syn-
dromes or death of the brain as a result of an oxygen shortage
exceeding the brain's resuscitation period. Since doctors usually
have to attempt reanimation suddenly and without warning,
they have to act immediately without being able to determine
the extent of oxygen loss to the brain. As a result their efforts
produce creatures which are irretrievably unconscious with
merely vegetative reactions and no capacity for mental experience. Continued artificial respiration and the use of the necessary
battery of intensive care techniques may then be able to maintain vital functions, even if in the long run complications from
infections of the lungs or urinary tracts, or general infection,
cannot be avoided and lead within weeks or months to a final
collapse of circulation and death. In the case of death of the

brain, this period is reduced to between two and five to six days. In this condition failure of a central mechanism controlling circulation and temperature leads to an irreversible fall in blood pressure and hypothermia, followed inevitably by cardiac arrest.

The cost of these procedures in equipment and personnel, together with the knowledge that there is no chance of meaningful revival, have led to the proposal that therapeutic measures should be abandoned when the prognosis shows no likelihood of benefit. The person who is unconscious and has no prospect of improvement has lost his individual personality and is eking out a purely biological, vegetative existence with controlled heart and circulation functions. The doctor's task of healing ends here with concern for the strain on close relatives and friends, and on nursing staff who could be more usefully employed in other ways. The problem is of particular concern to neuro-surgeons, who have to make decisions in cases of serious cranio-cerebral injuries and extensive brain tumours.

In this situation a distinction must be made between the irreversible loss of all brain functions—death of the brain—and all the states in which there is more or less serious damage to the cerebral cortex, but the brain stem continues to function—the apallic syndrome. In the latter, signs of life are reduced and unco-ordinated, but basically present. These patients must be regarded as human beings with a right to care. In a different category are the patients whose brains have died, who have to have continual artificial respiration and in whom a collapse of circulation cannot be remedied within a short time.

The ending of attempts at reanimation would also be crucial here because people whose brains have died are in demand as ideal donors for organ transplants. The removal of an organ from such a person would only be permissible, however, if death were certified in cases of brain death. This would be a convention. If the failure of brain function is regarded as more important than that of the heart, there is widespread agreement today that death should be defined by reference to the death of the brain as an organ. For this it is essential to show the irreversible loss of all brain functions before death can be certified in cases of death of the brain.

Since it is clear that the death of the brain is equivalent to a prognosis of complete death, the discussion has concentrated on the reliability of diagnostic parameters and ways of showing irreversible loss of all brain functions. Even serious cortical damage as part of an apallic syndrome is not the same as the death of the brain. These problems may now be regarded as solved.

V. Ascertainment of the Death of the Brain

To clarify the process of death in cases of death of the brain we will explain the pathogenesis of the process. If we take the previously mentioned example of reduction in the oxygen supply (hypoxia), we know from Hirsch's experimental models that even when the brain has been deprived of oxygen for a long period neuroglia cells can be shown to be alive even though there is no longer any sign of brain function. This means that we cannot rely on morphological criteria, but must base judgments on function. This is the practice implicit in the traditional signs of death, where cardiac arrest or the absence of breathing involved functional concepts, and determination of death did not have to wait for the morphological death of the last body cell.

There can be a loss of brain functions when, as a result of generalized damage of varying origin (toxic, vascular, traumatic, etc.), the brain and brain stem, and especially the vital centres, cease functioning. A breakdown of brain functions may also occur as a result of a breakdown in the connections between the brain and the brain stem or between the brain stem and the spinal cord, as a result of constriction due to changes in volume and weight (4). In both cases a clear clinical development can be traced. Brain damage rarely progresses so rapidly that the intermediate stages cannot be seen.

If brain damage goes further, however, there eventually occurs an irreversible cessation of all brain functions. This is distinguished from the bulbar syndrome stage by the permanent disappearance of vegetative functions. There are no definitive individual symptoms which permit a diagnosis of brain death, but the clinical picture of the death of the brain can be clearly outlined by reference to a constellation of symptoms involving the most important signs, deep coma with no reaction to strong external stimuli, absence of cerebral reflexes with dilated pupils which do not react to light, and central failure of automatic breathing. Nevertheless the clinical complex is not completely sure, because in some rare cases, such as severe heat loss or poisoning from sleeping drugs, a similar but reversible state occurs which could be confused with death of the brain on superficial observation without knowledge of the previous history. This means that for a sure diagnosis auxiliary investigations with instruments are needed, and these cannot be omitted even when the clinical picture appears conclusive.

Graphs of the electrical currents in the brain produced by an electro-encephalogram (EEG) show a characteristic alteration in the case of death of the brain. Whereas normally graphs show a variety of frequencies and rhythms, the characteristic of graphs in the case of brain death is complete electrical inactivity. This is called an iso-electric or, better, zero-line EEG (11). This method has become one of the most important auxiliary techniques, even though it reflects only the momentary state of the brain and allows no prognosis. Attempts have been made to confirm diagnoses by means of continuous or repeated electro-encephalograms, but the researchers were finally forced to admit that even after periods as long as seventy-two hours diagnostic certainty could not be achieved. The demonstrative value of a zero-line EEG does not increase with time, so that it is impossible to determine whether the disappearance of cerebral function will be reversible or irreversible. More important, an electro-encephalogram records only the activity of the cerebral cortex, and allows no conclusions about the functioning of sub-cortical brain structures. Penin has described a zero-line EEG as comparable to a frozen lake, in which currents are concealed under the ice.

Death of the brain cannot therefore be proved by an electro-encephalogram, but the use of this technique is essential to diagnosis, since a zero-line EEG is essential before the hypothesis of brain death can be considered. Even minimal or pathological electrical activity in the brain destroys the diagnosis. This gives electro-encephalography an important role as a front-line investigation technique.

Crucial in the diagnosis of brain death are typical changes in the brain vessels, which can be registered by angiography and prove the disappearance of function in the brain (13). It had been shown that the pathogenesis of brain death involves an increase in pressure within the skull as a result of brain oedema. This swelling of the brain can be observed to a lesser degree after any brain damage, but it can be of such proportions that the blood circulation in the brain is restricted. The first sign is a slowing down of the blood flow, until eventually, in extreme cases, cerebral blood circulation stops. X-ray pictures of the brain vessels can show a contrast medium as stationary, showing that the blood supply to the brain is completely cut off (2, 8). Since interruption of the cerebral blood circulation, depending on duration, leads to definable damage as a result of lack of oxygen, irreversible loss of brain function can be conclusively confirmed when the interruption of circulation lasts longer than the brain's resuscitation period of 8–10 minutes. Oedema indicates a final state, however, and the phase of complete interruption of the cerebral blood circulation is equivalent to total necrosis of the brain from ischaemia. This pathogenetic account is in complete agreement with the findings of neuropathologists. The brain as a whole is antolytic, with no inflammation reactions from the organism; it appears to be temporarily dissociated from the rest of the organism, atrophied.

When it was demonstrated that this pathogenesis applies not only to brain injuries but also to brain damage caused by lack of oxygen (7, 9), it was clear that—except for extensive destruction of the brain—death of the brain is not produced by the original cerebral damage, whether traumatic, from lack of oxygen or a symptom of poisoning, but by the subsequent brain oedema and the resulting complete interruption of the blood circulation of the brain. The time lapse required for the development of brain oedema can be traced clinically from brain damage to the appearance of the brain death syndrome.

The process of death is always gradual. It begins with the failure of the functions of vital systems of organs. Whatever the underlying complaint, in the end the last heartbeat is synonymous with the end of life; the ultimate cause of death is the failure of the action of the heart. Under the special conditions of reanimation, however, the process of death can be altered so that a clear decision is no longer possible, as when respirators take over the breathing and the circulation is supported by drugs. In such a situation cardiac arrest does not have the character of the definitive end of life. In these cases the higher criterion of intact, restorable or partially or totally irreversible loss of brain functions has proved appropriate. Death can be pronounced when the occurrence of brain death is confirmed by the irreversible loss of all brain functions.

Translated by Francis McDonagh

BIBLIOGRAPHY

1. Bichat, M. F. X., *Recherches physiologiques sur la vie et la mort* (Paris, 1800).
2. Bücheler, E., Käufer, C., Düx, A., "Zerebrale Angiographie zur Bestimmung des Hirntodes", *Fortschr. Röntgenstr.* 113 (1970, p. 278.
3. Fischgold, H., Mathis, D., "Obnubilations, comas, stupeurs", Études electrocéphalographiques", *Electroencéph. clin. Neurophysiol*, Supplement 11 (Paris, 1959).
4. Gerstenbrand, F., in Penin, H. and Käufer, C., *Der Hirntod* (Stuttgart, 1969).
5. Gütgemann, A., Käufer, C., "Der Scheintod", *Dtsch. med. Wschr.* 95 (1970), p. 702.
6. Hirsch, H. Gleichmann, U., Kristen, H., Magazinovic, V., "Über die Beziehung zwischen O_2-Aufnahme des Gehirns und O_2-Druck im Sinusblut bei uneingeschränkter und eingeschränkter Durchblutung", *Pflügers Arch. Ges. Physiol.* 273 (1961), p. 213.
7. Käufer, C., *Die Bestimmung des Todes bei irreversiblem Verlust der Hirnfunktionen* (Heidelberg, 1971).
8. Käufer, C., Bücheler, E., "Hirntod und Organtransplantation", *Dtsch. med. J.* 22 (1971), p. 185.
9. Käufer, C., Penin, H., Düx, A., Kersting, G., Schneider, H., and Kubicki, S., "Zerebraler Zirkulationsstillstand bei Hirntod durch Hypoxydosen", *Fortschr. Med.* (1969), p. 713.
10. Mollaret, P., Goulon, M., "Le coma dépassé. Mémoire préliminaire", *Rev. Neurol.* 101 (1959), p. 3.
11. Penin, H., Käufer, C., *Der Hirntod* (Stuttgart, 1969).
12. Schneider, M., "Überlebens—und Wiederlebenszeit von Gehirn, Herz, Leber, Niere nach Ischaemie und Anoxie" (Cologne and Opladen, 1965).
13. Tönnis, W., Frowein, R. A., "Wie lange ist Wiederbelebung bei schweren Hirnverletzungen möglich?", *Mschr. Unfallheilkunde* 66 (1963), p. 169.
14. Wawersik, J., "Kriterien des Todes", *Studium Generale* 23 (1970), p. 319.

Luciano Caglioti

Human Survival and Individual Death

THE rapid development of science over the last few decades has radically altered man's attitude to life and his relationships with others. Obviously even his mode of thinking is changing and it can be said that the greatest effort required of man in techno- logical society is to adapt his own personality to the enormous quantity of information and instruments which the world he lives in places at his disposal or forces upon him. This difficulty is not only experienced by the man in the street but also by the scientist, who finds himself facing the problem of assembling the new discoveries of science in a synthesis that he finds manageable.

This is a particularly difficult question for students of quantum mechanics. They can link mathematically quantities like energy and matter. They can predict by mathematical calculations the existence of elementary subatomic particles which then turn out to exist in fact. They can even verify the possibilities of the existence of anti-matter, but, because they think mathematically, they encounter great difficulty in fitting such realities into an "anthropomorphic" scheme. During the sixties, the strenuous efforts of biologists to establish the molecular bases of life have been crowned by increasing success. Here also, however, the solution of one problem opens others and biologists—and especi- ally molecular biologists—pursue the ultimate secret of life, which is always within reach but always escapes from their understanding. The successes obtained nevertheless constitute a general basis for present society.

Anyone who endeavours to face up to the problem of man, anyone who in the seventies tries to reply to the question "Who are we?", which Plotinus asked, cannot do without certain factual data furnished by biology.

No philosophy which investigates man can be opposed to the discoveries of biological science, but must take them into account.

The complex range of data which has been acquired on the evolutionary origin of man constitutes an important basis for students. The theory of evolution, founded on Darwin's intuition, is by now universally accepted by scientists. This result has been reached after many studies which led to the acquisition of valid scientific proofs, and much controversy. Indeed, Darwin's theory has not had an easy life and scientists who were convinced of its truth have often met the hostility of the world around them. That hostility was particularly profound on the part of those who objected to the intolerable conflict between evolutionary theories and other explanations of a more traditional kind about the origin of man.

Caution with regard to new ideas (and in this case the novelty was very striking) was complicated by another factor: the proofs of Darwin's theory, based on the finding of fossils, were sometimes challenged even by dispassionate observers. A common objection was the so-called missing link. It can be understood how persons belonging to different cultural milieux and sometimes wielding great authority have let themselves indulge, at times in a rather incautious way, in drastic condemnations of an idea.

Modern biochemistry and genetics have provided convincing proofs of the theory of evolution. There has been strikingly successful classification of the mechanism by which the information contained in the molecules of living organisms is conveyed. This mechanism is the same for all organisms and it has revealed a unity in the biological world which is perfectly in accord with the evolutionary theory.

Of particular interest in this context is the study of the sequences of amino-acids in proteins which are found in different organisms developing, as is the case with cytochromes, the same chemical function. A protein is constituted by the random succession of twenty different amino-acids. The total number of amino-acid units in a cytochrome is about 110, so that a cytochrome can be considered as a word composed of twenty different letters combined among themselves in random fashion up to a total length of 110 letters. The investigation, carried out with the help of a computer, of the sequences of amino-acids which make up the individual proteins originating from different organisms has enabled a phylogenetic pedigree to be drawn up which to a great extent coincides with the hypothesis of Darwin and his followers which was based on the study of fossil finds.[1]

The coincidence between the sequences of haemoglobin in the gorilla and in man is particularly striking. Among 146 amino-acids only one variation has been found, which is to say that two sequences can be superimposed over 20^{146} possibilities. There are repeated manifestations of this unity in the biological world. For example, many poisons are universal, and even many drugs. All hormones extracted from animals, except for a few protected on grounds of immunology, can be administered to man. Even at the level of behaviour, drugs and medicines can induce similar reactions in the animal and in man. An extreme example is LSD which provokes hallucinations in man, and induces spiders to spin "hallucinatory" cobwebs.

We have said that it can be affirmed that man is the result of an evolutionary process, just as all living beings on earth are the result of evolution. That is, they are the result of a process which has selected, among the various species, those better adapted to survive (many in fact have become extinct) and, among the individuals of the same species, those better adapted to survive. The process is continuous and universal. Every living being is continually subject to checks on the validity of its own requisites for survival. Every living being, in other words, shares in the struggle for existence. Observation of the animal world demonstrates the extreme complexity of the mechanisms which permit survival of animal species. These mechanisms have been established by means of a fierce process of selection, which has suppressed the less well adapted individuals and respected those better adapted. The behaviour of animals is in accord with one

[1] M. O. Daghoff, "Computer Analysis of Protein Evolution", *Scientific American* (June 1969).

primary purpose—survival. The sexual instinct, the care of offspring, the search for food, the flight from danger—all these belong to the heritage, partly innate, partly acquired, with which the animal confronts the struggle for existence. In this respect, the collective suicide of lemmings is an exceptional case, apparently in contrast with the instinct of preservation, and it is naturally the object of considerable study.

The evolution of the human race is the result of two components, one biological and one cultural. Cultural evolution has had an extraordinary importance on effects of the survival of the human race. Among two million species, ours is the only one to possess a symbolic language, to have consciousness of self and of death and the ability to hand on culture and to regulate personal behaviour according to that culture. (For a complete and fascinating treatment of these questions, see the works of T. Dobzhansky.)

Man faces the struggle for existence with a unique genetic and cultural heritage. Among man's various tendencies, such as attachment to children, love of the family, the wish to associate and the capacity to learn and communicate with symbolic language, the tendency to survive is undoubtedly very strong. What part has this tendency played in the evolution of the human species and to what extent has it gone on increasing in strength as a consequence of natural selection?

It seems legitimate to admit that in the course of evolution those beings, which were in other respects equal but had a less marked tendency to survive, have been step by step eliminated more than others. If that has been verified, if individuals who wish to survive are selected, then the tendency to survive has itself been selected and strengthened, and is therefore at the same time both the cause and the effect of a positive biological evolution of the human species.

The result of this process is that we feel in our hearts, like a potent natural law, an attachment to life. In the light of the above considerations it is unthinkable that man should be characterized by indifference to death or by the wish to die. He would not have survived, just as the human species would have died out if mothers had been characterized by a tendency to abandon the newly-born.

Man, we have said, is the only animal to possess conscious-ness both of himself and of the inevitability of death. At the same time, man has been selected through a mechanism by which his whole being tends to survive. To what extent is conflict produced by this consciousness of self and tendency to survive on the one hand and consciousness of death on the other? Grief for death is well known to Western man. As Simonides of Chios said, "Death is inevitable and hangs over us." Two thousand years later, Dobzhansky said that "Man is burdened with death-awareness. A being who knows that he will die arose from ancestors who did not know".[2] Also, the same author stressed, "having become aware of the inevitability of death, man has tasted the Forbidden Fruit."[3] That grief is the bill which the individual, with his consciousness of himself, pays, as if by an original vice, for the survival of the human race.

Cult of the dead, which is widespread throughout human society, and certainty or hope that the soul is immortal or that there are other forms of survival after death are a source of comfort for man. Apart from religious beliefs, it has also com-forted man to link the moment of death to a noble or glorious action—"It is glorious for a virtuous man to have died either falling in the front ranks in battle or fighting for his fatherland" (Tyrtaeus) or else—a rather uncommon practice—to dull con-sciousness with drugs. Meanwhile, at another level, great un-certainty is felt by the philosopher, the scientist or the theologian when he is called to choose between euthanasia and keeping mechanically alive a body that is mindless or a prey to irrever-sible suffering; or between procreation, a natural instinct for animal and man, and birth-control, a demand of society: that is, when the reason examines problems which touch closely on the intimate mechanisms of the evolution of the human species.

Translated by J. P. Donnelly

[2] T. Dobzhansky, *The Biology of Ultimate Concern* (New York, 1967; London 1969), p. 69.
[3] *Ibid,,* pp. 76–7.

Elisabeth Kübler-Ross

Dying as a Human-Psychological Event

MUCH has been written about our dying patients"[1,2] need for further communications during this final crisis. As medicine and science have progressed, adding more years to the lifespan of men, we have been faced with new and more difficult human problems. The issues of prolongation of life, dying with dignity, as well as the patient's rights in regard to these decisions poses new dilemmas.

Marya Mannes, in the excellent essay, *Last Rights*,[3] states: "Find the answer or be devoured." Essentially we attempted to seek the answer when we started our seminars on death and dying approximately eight years ago. It was initiated originally by several theology students who were asked to write a paper on crisis in human life. They chose dying as the greatest human crisis men had to face. When I was approached for help, we soon decided that we should ask those most intimately involved, namely, dyng patients themselves. This led to a series of interviews with critically ill patients and ultimately, to an accredited year-long course on "Death and Dying" for medical and theology students, nurses, social workers, and other members of the helping profession.

We asked dying patients to be our teachers. Appreciating that someone was still interested in them, and having the need for

[1] *On Death and Dying*, Elisabeth Kübler-Ross (New York, 1969).
[2] *Questions and Answers on Death and Dying*, Elisabeth Kübler-Ross (New York, 1974).
[3] *Last Rights*, Marya Mannes (New York, 1974).

human contacts and communications, they gladly volunteered to assist us. We interviewed hundreds of terminally ill patients in a one-way screened interviewing area. Immediately afterwards, an interdisciplinary team discussed the interview in order to familiarize ourselves with our own reactions as well as to come to terms with our own fears and conflicts in facing these patients.

The following paper summarizes briefly some of the highlights of the lessons from these dying patients.

Despite the fact that physicians and health personnel were opposed to our project, and often went so far as to deny the existence of dying patients in their wards, the patients themselves were quite relieved when we approached them with our request. Many were bitter about the "conspiracy of silence", the lack of open and honest discussions and their resulting inability to "put their house in order".

We were most impressed that they "knew" that they were dying and that they were able to convey to us when death was close. I wish to emphasize that patients are aware of their impending death even if they have not been informed of the seriousness of their illness. Further, it has been my experience that young children "protected" by parents and the staff, who were unable to face the impending death of the child, likewise were aware of their impending death.

Patients pass through certain adjustment reactions, which I call the stages of dying. It has to be understood that not all patients go through these stages and certainly do not pass through these stages in this order. In general, however, most patients, adults more than children, respond initially with shock and denial. They believe "it shall happen to thee and to thee, but not to me". Even the less than one per cent of our patients who remained in the stage of denial until their death were able to tell us about their awareness of their impending death. These patients, however, use a symbolic language to communicate this awareness to us. A young woman, who was rejected by her husband and left three pre-school children behind, was unable to face this grim reality, and was convinced that God had cured and healed her. A few days prior to her actual death, I sat with her in silence holding her hand, when she suddenly whispered,

"I hope that when my hands get colder and colder, I hope I have warm hands like yours holding mine". In our interpretation, this patient talked about her imminent death, simply requesting the presence of a caring human being during her last hours of life. A social worker described beautifully the result of our own inability to face the death of a young patient; she recalled her first traumatic visit to a dying man who was her own age; "I knew he wanted to talk to me, but I always turned it into something light ... a little joke, or some evasive reassurance which had to fail. The patient knew, and I knew, but as the patient felt my anxiety, he kept to himself what he wanted to share with another human being ... and so he died and did not bother me."

A patient quickly senses who is able to talk with him. He will only "play the game" and keep silent with those who cannot face reality. All of our patients have been able to convey to us three basic communications; *when* they need help, *from whom* they wish assistance, and *what* it is they need. When a terminally ill patient says "Please sit down now", it is imperative that we spend some time with him *now* ... and not tomorrow ... because tomorrow may be too late. Patients also choose with whom they wish to share their final needs. We cannot and should not impose our services on them. I was reminded of this vividly on one of my last visits to a middle-aged dying woman, prior to my leaving the University hospital. Because of my own needs, I repeated my rounds twice on that day in an attempt to have all my terminally ill patients taken care of prior to my departure. This patient impressed me by her deep sadness and inability to relate any specific needs. I left her with the distinct feeling that my visit was to no avail. When I returned a few hours later, after lunchtime, to my astonishment the patient had a content smile on her face. I asked her about the change in her mood, and she made the following statement: "You know, today over lunchtime, my favourite nurse walked into the room. She was always so damned professional. But today, at twelve o'clock, she came in here and just stood at the end of the bed, without saying or doing anything. Then I suddenly noticed tears rolling down her cheeks. She became embarrassed and left quickly." In almost disbelief, I said, "And that is all you had to see?"; she responded, "Yes; you see, she was always my favourite nurse. I had to be sure that she *cared*." I hope that examples like this make it clear that no other staff person could have helped this patient more than this "favourite nurse", who, without any verbal expressions, was able to show her true feelings of sorrow and grief for this patient, and thus communicated her love and care for this patient.

If a critically ill patient has one human being who is able to talk about realistic issues, the patient is then able to drop his denial and often proceeds through a stage of anger and rage. This is when the patient criticizes doctors, nurses, visitors, food, procedures, and tests. He is often an artist in making us both guilty and angry, thus provoking more isolation and loneliness at a time when he needs our help the most. We have to be aware that their anger is often a simple cry, "Why me?" If we learn not to take all of their anger personally, but rather as an expression of their anguish, we may be able to help him to express this rage, rather than blaming and "punishing" him by further isolation and withdrawal. Perhaps the most difficult patients are the young adults, who are just beginning to live when "their future is taken away from them". Much too often we send them get well cards when we know all too well that they are not getting well. All too often, parents and friends talk to them about future projects which will never materialize. The patient knows ... and we know; but because of our own needs to keep up this pretence, the dying patient is too weary and annoyed to pursue the game. The patient, therefore, withdraws, becomes monosyllabic and displays his anger to anyone who enters his room with a cheerful smile or an energetic step. All these people, naturally, remind him of the things he is in the process of losing.

Family members pass through the same anger; they may question God; "Why do you let this happen to my child?" Needless to say, we should accept the patients' anger as well as the anger of families. We should help them to express their rage, even if it is displaced on to the staff or God. If we can understand these people rather than judge or label them, we may be successful in helping them to the next stage ... the stage of bargaining. During the phase of bargaining, the patient appears calm and composed, almost as if he were at peace. It is well to know that this is only a temporary truce. The patient is now able to acknowledge that it is happening to him, but he pleads (usually with God) for a little extension of time "to finish unfinished business".

This is our last chance, for members of the health profession and family members, to assist him to put his house in order, to make a last will, or concern himself with the care of children that might be left behind. This is also the time when a patient may wish to make that long dreamed of voyage or visit with friends, that has always been postponed. When the bargaining time is up, the patient enters the depression stage. The patient first mourns past losses, talks about the loss of a limb or a job, or simply grieves that he cannot stay at home with his family. He then stops relating verbally, and enters the period of silent, preparatory grief, in which he begins to mourn future losses. It is during this silent grief period that the healthy people in his environment begin to have problems. We tolerate silent grief poorly, and we respond to a crying man all too often with the superficial encouragement to "cheer up".

It is strange that we allow a widow to grieve for a year when she loses *one* beloved person, but we show little empathy when a man cries, who after all shows courage in facing the impending loss of everything and everybody he has ever loved! We encourage our patients to cry and help them not to feel "unmanly or cowardly" during this time of separation and decathoxis. We respect his needs to see less visitors, to reduce the laboratory tests to an absolute minimum and, if humanly possible, to allow him to die at home rather than in an institution.

If we can accept our patients' needs and do not project our own needs (the need to prolong life at all costs, the need to hang on to a dying husband, implicitly conveying to him, "Don't die on me") the dying person will then reach the final stage of true acceptance. He is without fear and anguish, often with minimal pain and simply expressing his comfort by a silent pressing of the hand and a statement, perhaps, "My time is very close and it is all right". Tolstoy perhaps knew this final acceptance when he described Ilyich in his final moments of life, saying, "In place of death, there was light"; then Ilyich proclaimed, "So that's what it is! What joy!" Then he muttered, "It is finished, Death is finished. . . ."

Anyone who has passed through this valley of shadows with his patients has experienced this great sense of peace and perhaps even accomplishment. When our patients pass from this life, it should always be remembered that we too, the members of the helping profession, experience a great sense of peace and accomplishment when we have been able to stay with these patients from the initial stage of denial, through the periods of testing and anger, through the times of tears and mourning, to this final feeling of victory and acceptance.

Nobody better than dying patients themselves will ultimately help us work through our own fears and help us to reach the acceptance of our own finiteness, hopefully, years before we have to die. This is their gift to us, if we do not desert them in the time of this crisis.

Garrett Barden

Study of the Ritual
Representation of Death[1]

YOU are ready to leave me now. Do not look back; look ahead as you have been told. We live here as long as we are supposed to. Never wish for us to hasten and join you, for you will find your brothers there and your mother and father and grandparents. Do not trouble us. We will do all you requested before you died.

This burial prayer of the Cjibwa of North America represents three aspects of death and concentrates on the first of these: the concern of the living to rid themselves completely of the dead; their concern for the welfare of the dead; the transitional journey.

Robert Hertz in his essay of 1907 was the first to draw attention to the universality of the idea that the dead are in some fashion still among the living until, by appropriate rites, they are finally cut off and sent to the community of the dead. This idea has three important consequences. It involves the idea that death is more than putrefaction and decay and so allows for a differentation between human and non-human death. It implies that the human person (and, in some cases, certain animals too, e.g. elephant and cattle among the Sudanese Nuer) is in some sense continuous. Finally, it involves the representation of the place of the dead and hence the opposition between the place of the living and that of the dead.

[1] I am indebted to my friend Dr Eric ten Raa of the University of Western Australia and to my friend Mrs Frances Dorr of my own university for helpful comments on a draft of this essay.

Exclusive concentration on this aspect of death is unusual once the ritual is understood as something more than the mere remedy for personal and social felt loss. Doubtless there is personal and communal grief at death and this grieving is incorporated into funeral rites but there is, I believe, no community for which death is no more than an occasion for grief. This is true even with the attenuated ritual observances of a contemporary industrial society. Death is more than material decay; it pollutes because it is dangerous. Death is represented as releasing into another realm an element in the human that is variously translated as spirit, soul, ghost, shadow (though in the last case it would seem that there is here analogy or metaphor rather than the idea that the shadow thrown on the wall by the sun is one's soul or spirit). The spirit released by death is now wandering among the living but in a fearful way. The funeral rite exists to send the dead finally away. The community may not be very interested in the place to which the spirit goes; none the less, that place is now present in their cosmogony and is available for further reflection. Thus the exorcism of the spirit introduces an intellectual unease into the community.

The ritual is effective inasmuch as it causes the spirit to leave the domain of the living. (Ritual need not be thought of as mechanically effective; it is rather a kind of speech that the wandering spirit must obey or, as we shall consider later, the kind of speech that the spirit requires in order to cross the line from one domain to the other.) As can be seen from the Ojibwa prayer, the speech of ritual may be persuasive—the spirit is given reasons why it should depart. Ritual, thus, presents the place of the spirit and so becomes a way of knowledge which includes within itself a demand for its development.

A shift of emphasis comes with concentration on the welfare of the dead. This shift is seen in the expansion of the description of the abode of the dead. When before it was merely a place, now it is a place with its own time. The ritual discovers human death as revealing the dimensions of human time, for not only is death the conclusion of a life but it shows that that life always had a conclusion. This aspect remains hidden as long as the ritual concentrates on the reintegration and purification of social life since there is an apparent timelessness about the survival of the community.

Concentration on the welfare of the dead leads to the question about the temporality of the dead by way of the simple and obvious question as to whether or not the dead will die again. Because time and place are so closely allied the second death of the dead involves either a further place or their return—as in a cosmogony of reincarnation—into the world of the living. (The incessant wandering of the dead in some cosmogonies is the equivalent of a sequence of deaths since the time of wandering is the time of continual dying seen as transition; the second death of the Apocalypse represents its finality.)

Again, concentration on the welfare of the dead and on the temporal nature of their place inclines the community to think of this place and life as passing away. This is so much a commonplace of the so-called High Religions that its non-obvious quality is obscured. No doubt it is obvious that men die but the transitoriness of society as a whole is by no means obvious (indeed, the opposite seems more obvious!) and as long as the ritual concentrates on the removal of the dead from the world of living it is the persistence, and not at all the transcience, of human society that is represented.

When ritual expands the description of the place and time of the dead, then, over against the world of the living, the world of the dead appears as survival over against transcience. The ritual now represents the finitude, not of the dead person, nor even of the mourners, but of human life. From the acknowledgment of individual mortality, the communal representation moves to the acknowledgment of mortality as constitution of life.

The ritual, then, contrasts two modes of living or being, that of the living which is mortal and that of the dead which is immortal. Tales of the origin of death fit nicely here, for it is a strange feature of such stories that many have little to do with people dying, and even when they do feature people dying the burden of the story has to do with the living. In the epic of Gilgamesh, for instance, the hero travels to the land of Utnapishtim, where he finds the flower of eternal life which he loses when crossing a river on his way home. Henceforward, Gilgamesh is under sentence of death and not only he, nor even every single person, but the community, for the eponymous ancestor stands not for each single individual but for the community and for the individual as a member of the community.

Among the Sanpoil of North America the story of the origin of death includes the death of two of the chief protagonists—a girl and her brother who had committed incest together. Still, it is not their death that is the origin of death for, as the myth states, their death was not yet definitive; it was in their father's power to resurrect them. However, his fellows forbade him to do so and, in revenge, being a powerful sorcerer, killed their children too. Now they begged him to bring back all the children to life but by this time his own son and daughter were decomposed and so beyond his power and he refused to do so. The father says: Henceforth death shall be irrevocable. What is important in this story is not so much that some have died but that death is now the fate of the living.

In this Sanpoil myth is another very widespread association: the origin of death is linked with some fault, whether serious or slight. There are, of course, several faults mentioned in the myth, e.g. the original incest, the father's punishment of the son by killing him, the daughter's subsequent suicide, the father's colleagues' refusal to allow him to resurrect his son and daughter, his consequent killing of their children by sorcery, but beneath them all is what we may call the ontological fault. The irrevocability of death is not properly a punishment for all these faults but is rather the inevitable result of the state of affairs that these faults have brought into being; when the father is finally entreated to restore the children to life it is already too late—the corpses of his own children are rotting. Similarly, in many East African myths, death is not so much punishment for a fault as the inevitable result of the fault. Evans-Pritchard, in his book *Nuer Religion,* refers to this characteristic as the Oedipal quality of the origin of death; the reference to a great tragedy may counterbalance the modern tendency to consider the ritual thinking of death as trivial.

With the expansion (whether this was historical or logical) of the description of the abode of the dead came the contrast between the abode of the living and that of the dead and the quest for the origin of death which, in its turn, sets up the contrast between this life presided over by death and another original life in which death did not exist. Stories of the origin of death propose reasons for the transition from this original state to the present. In this context the slightness of the fault is not trivial since what is to be explained is what appears as an inevitability that was not inevitable. It is, I think, for this reason that the original representation of the source of death is not moral, for the moral is not, properly speaking, inevitable. Therefore, to explain a life that is presided over by death—understood as a falling away from an original perfection—there is introduced a flaw with inevitable consequences. The crimes of Oedipus were no doubt great but the tragedy is not in his sin but in the inevitable consequences of what were, initially, perfectly avoidable events— indeed, in the eyes of their perpetrator, Oedipus, not sins at all. A modern moral sense tends to read the story of Adam and Eve in the garden as simple disobedience and to neglect that their state after having eaten the fruit was the inevitable concomitant consequence of their new knowledge. It is true that they were driven out of the garden but already they were separated from their original conversation with God. By eating the fruit, they changed the state of things. By allowing time to pass and the bodies to decompose the father in the Sanpoil story allowed the state of things to change.

Consideration of the finitude of human life has led to the consideration of the original existence but to no further understanding of the state that exists among the dead. The original state had in itself the possibility of decline (since the present is in fact a declension from it) and if the dead were to return to that original state there could be an incessant repetition of the decline. Thus, in some Indian cosmogonies death in one period or age is merely the entry into the next when the original time will return to be followed by a subsequent declension. There seems no way out of the interminable circle except by final damnation or salvation. (Total extinction is, of course, structurally, either one.)

This may seem an unduly logical approach but in its basic patterns ritual thinking is logical. Its non-logical areas are, as it were, the places for its advancement. The community may not, in practice, consider the well-being of the dead—the problem may be passed over—but if it turns to the problem at all, then it will find that the ritual provides basic guidelines for, in the ritual, the community has gone further than it knew.

In the stories of the origin of death the crucial element is a transition from an original perfection to an imperfect present. This transition is rarely made by death but through some flaw to the state presided over by death. But death as it now exists, and the death of the individual, is universally thought of as a transition. It was suggested above that one of the functions of the funeral rite is to dispatch the spirit from the realm of the living to that of the dead. It is not, then, primarily physical death that is the transition, for the spirit's escape from the corpse in death leaves it free to roam about the domain of the living but not yet able to enter the domain of the dead. The ritual has, therefore, the enabling function of conducting the spirit to its proper domain; the spirit is removed from the living by virtue of its being initiated into the realm of the dead.

The ritual here sets itself a further problem: who is competent to conduct the spirit? Almost everywhere the problem is solved by the establishment of ritual specialists (a priesthood or shamanhood) with appropriate education but nowhere is the ritual specialist sufficient. There is always a superhuman being who can be invoked by the shaman and who will conduct the spirit to its place. In the ritual the spirit is both asked to go and the conductor is asked to lead it. Thus, among the Ojibwa, *Otter* may be asked to take the spirit on his back and among the Nuer the high God is asked to take away the man he has made. It is worth noting that the mood of ritual here is request rather than command; this mood is linked to the need for a superhuman power.

Among many communities, death is used as a metaphor for other important transitions, e.g. among the Ngatatjara of Central Australia the first part of the initiation ritual in which the boy becomes a man is devoted to the initiand's dying to his former life of childhood. Reflection on the structure of such actions reveals the ritual structure of dying itself. There is an initial break or separation which is often represented in physical distance, darkness, lack of communication, followed by a period of tests and other ritual preparations. Likewise the spirit may be thought to go through a number of trials or temptations before finally being brought to its last resting place. Again, as the boy requires the ritual talk to become a man, so the spirit requires the ritual of the funeral to become a member of the community of the dead.

In contrast to an individualist morality and an individualist life and death, human death ritual—that is, the ways in which men have conceived death—has, for the most part, stressed the communal character of the basic human actions. So the ritual is the journey of the spirit. The well-known insistence that the ritual be carried out at the right time, in the right place and in the right manner is related to this fact. Thus, among the Sandawe of Tanzania, the rituals are associated with the movements of the sun and the phases of the moon—the sun being associated with death because of its sudden disappearance at night. This insistence has in the past been interpreted by Europeans as a sort of mechanical magic but recent researches into the operation of language have to some extent brought about a better appreciation of ritual action. The spirit is, as it were, talked through the hazards of its journey and its conductor or guide is asked to lead it rightly. An individualistic culture asks why the guide might not do this by itself but the ritual conception of the human includes the consideration that the spirit achieves its journey as a member of a community, not as an isolated individual, and the ritual itself enacts that community.

The passage from the world of the living to that of the dead is dangerous (a feature shared with significant transitions in other spheres) and difficult and often, even when there is a developed conception of the next life, there is the possibility of the spirit failing to make the transition properly—the ghost in European thought is an example of this. Transition, then, is an incomplete action, a movement to a goal, which may remain unfulfilled inasmuch as the goal is not reached. The essential incompleteness of passage evokes more precisely the question of the nature of the goal which will now be conceived in the ritual precisely as goal.

In communities where a developed ritual image of the abode of the dead has been worked out, this abode seems to be evaluated as (i) wholly good and desirable, e.g. the Christian heaven, the Buddhist *nirvāna;* (ii) wholly repugnant, e.g. the Christian hell; (iii) ambiguously undesirable, e.g. the early Jewish Sheol, the Classical Hades; the Christian Limbo. Some very tentative remarks ´about the inter-relations of these three may be made. The wholly repugnant abode (ii) never, to my knowledge, exists on its own in any cosmogony. It is always the negation of the wholly desirable place (i) and is often the development in the negative direction of the ambiguous (iii), e.g. the pit of the Apocalypse is developed in contrast to the New Jerusalem and is the negative development of Sheol. Contrariwise, a wholly desirable state can exist without its negative counterpart. Subsequent theological reflections in Christianity on hell as loss, absence, negation, are, then, the specification in another mode of knowing of what is already ritually known.

The ambiguously undesirable state may be compared with the transitional journey. I remarked that the transitional journey is an incomplete action not merely in the sense that sometimes the passage may not be successfully completed but more basically that the completion of the action is in its goal not in itself. I want to say now that the ambiguous state is often imagined as a passage —there is restlessness, wandering, ceaseless movement, in short, incompletion. The endless duration of this state is a scourge because it is finitude, i.e. temporal closure, that lends completion to this life. This is true even if the duration of society is not regarded as coming to an end since history is never merely a chronicle of endless events but sequences of significant plots. Aristotle's seemingly simplistic remarks concerning the beginning, middle and end of tragic action may be applicable to the way in which ritual discloses human living and characterizes the ambiguous abode of the dead by their absence.

It is clear that the ritual of death is a way of dealing with death; it is everywhere an effective action. Its mood is, as it were, imperative and invitatory. But it is also a mode of knowledge. The rite expresses the community's understanding of death but, because it pretends to an ontological dimension, the meaning of the rite goes beyond the actual meaning of the participants so that they may learn by reflection on it.

What is learnt by reflecting on ritual? This is the hermeneutical problem. I do not think that what is learnt is what the inventors of the ritual meant—it may be possible to penetrate to the meaning of the original authors of the rite but this meaning is not the meaning of the rite. Furthermore, the participants live in their own meaning which is evoked by their participation but this meaning, while it is a sharing in the meaning of the rite, is not yet the meaning of the rite, for the participants know that they can learn by meditating on the ritual. (It is worth noting that when one speaks of reflection on death one means reflection on the ritual conception of death. To refuse the tradition totally or rather to attempt to do so would be to attempt to attain an unattainable primeval blankness. This is so of all societies for the existence of none, that is the basic conceptions of none, is without tradition.)

I have tried to show that every ritual move has a meaning that is presently available to the participant but further that ritual sets problems that are potentially but not, perhaps, proximately available to him. The communal ritual is present in the community like a chess game the implications of whose moves are as yet unknown.

This reflection on ritual is not something quite other than its proper performance but the concept of reflection within ritual may shed some light on what proper performance might be. There is a widespread contemporary view that proper performance necessarily involves more than contemplative presence. This is a view akin to the idea in theatre that there should be no spectators but that all should be actors. It is a view that has neither historical nor trans-cultural validity. It overlooks the essential fact of the rite that it exists to be contemplated and is, perhaps, based on a concept of rite as primarily emotive. Yet even in the ritual of death, within which emotive grief is incorporated, the ritual expression of grief is not the spontaneous—although even still, cultural—overflow of grief but the representation of the knowledge of the place of grief in the whole cosmogony. Because this is so, grief and joy may be placed side by side in a way that would be impossible for the participant to feel in another mode.

Human death is a cultural experience. In the ritual of death the fundamental problem is not, primarily, what does death mean? but, rather, what problems does death pose? Because the problem is posed in this way the ritual solution is indefinitely expandable. This consideration of human death as it appears in ritual seems to indicate that recurrently in human society the problem of death is ontological and only secondarily emotive or moral.

Jacques-Marie Pohier

Death, Nature and Contingency

Anthropological Reflections about
the Postponement of Death

IN this article, we shall consider the problems that arise in connection with the possibilities that exist today of postponing the death of dying people by medical means and the various views of life and death which determine attitudes with regard to these problems. Most of the readers of *Concilium* belong to the social groups within which these problems arise in their most acute form. It is therefore important at the outset to bear in mind that, just as these problems did not arise for thousands of years simply because there were no medical means of slowing down the course of fatal diseases, they do not arise in 1974, as far as the majority of the world's population is concerned, mainly because these people cannot benefit from medical science. What is more, it has been proved statistically that, where health services exist, the economically less favoured classes are in a different situation with regard to medical assistance at the time of death from financially better off classes and that country or small-town dwellers are not in the same position as the inhabitants of large towns. There are, of course, many other factors which play a part, among the most important being the level of education and the profession followed. We may, however, conclude that the problems arising in the context of the possible postponement of death are recent and those confined to people in a more favourable situation.

This is, however, no reason for not considering them. It is to be hoped and indeed expected that those problems will arise for an increasing number of people. We are therefore bound to

question the various views of life and death which play a part
in determining these problems. It should not be forgotten that,
for man, death is not a right, but a datum of his nature. It is,
however, also part of man's nature that his death should be as
human as possible, as closely as possible in accordance with
what makes him human. Man has, in other words, the duty
in some way to be the principle and the agent of this human
action, if it is true that man is the image of God to the extent
that "he is the principle of his own actions, thanks to the will
and the power that he exercises when acting".[1] This inequality
of man in confrontation with death gives rise to two scandals.
In the first place, many people find it impossible to live their
lives—and therefore their deaths—in a human way. In the
second place, there is the scandal of death itself.

I

In the context of this particular issue of *Concilium*, our
problem arises most clearly in the case of a sick person who
develops a fatal illness. Although nothing more can be done
by medical means to ensure that he does not have to undergo
this illness or to suffer the death that results from it, it is not
true to say that nothing more can be done for him by medical
means. Medicine can in fact perform three functions here.

(1) It can certainly relieve the dying person's suffering and
everyone will agree that this may well be a right possessed by
the sick person and his relatives and by the doctor and nurses.
There are, however, problems involved here, the most important being whether the medical care should lead to unconsciousness. Has the dying person not the right to choose the possibility
of continuing to have relationships with those who surround
him (his family, other patients, the visiting priest and the
hospital staff) and above all with himself in preference to being
relieved from pain and being at the same time reduced to a
degree of unconsciousness? Because of his rights and duties, is
the doctor in charge entitled to deprive the sick person of this
right? A related problem is that of keeping the dying person

---

[1] Thomas Aquinas, *Summa Theologica*, prologue to Pars IIa.

in hospital, when he may prefer to die at home, in an environment which is more in accordance with the way he lived. Has the dying person not the right to choose this way of dying and has the doctor the right to make this choice for him?

(2) Medicine can shorten the time of dying. Leaving the question of euthanasia aside, it is possible to treat a dying patient in such a way that his suffering will be relieved, but that his resistance to death will be decreased. It is also possible to discontinue treatment, especially if it seems to be useless.[2] We are bound to ask here whether the doctor alone is competent to judge and whether the dying person should not be more entitled to decide or, if he cannot, those who surround him.

(3) It is also possible for death to be delayed by means of surgical, chemical or radiological treatment which may at the same time involve other serious risks. Everything depends in this case on the quality of life made possible during the time gained by delaying death in this way. Is the dying person bound to choose a treatment which will certainly postpone his death, but which will at the same time also lead to serious physical or psychical disablement? Has the doctor the right to decide for him? There are also various ways of delaying death by making good the defects or absence of an essential organ, such as the kidneys, a lung or the heart. Only the brain cannot at present be replaced in this way. Here too, the decisive factor must be the quality of life afterwards. The problem is posed in its most acute form in the case of irreversible arrest of cerebral activity.[3]

In all these cases, the chief problem is that of the rights and duties of each of the people concerned—the dying person, those who surround him and the doctor in charge of the patient. There may be a conflict not only inwardly in each of the individuals, but also between the individuals concerned. The problem, however, is not simply confined to these individuals. The different medical procedures involved are frequently carried

---

[2] The Church's teaching office has always acknowledged the rights of the sick person and of the doctor to decide in such cases. See, for example, Pius XII's allocution on analgesia, given on 24 February 1954 to doctors and surgeons.

[3] See C. Käufer's article in this issue of *Concilium*.

out by many highly skilled people and call for a high degree of responsibility and decision-making which must be based on a sound policy with regard to health and above all its economics. Even if such a policy were so utopian in theory that it would satisfy all the demands of the gospel and of justice in the widest sense, we are bound to recognize that there could never be sufficient doctors, nurses, instruments and hospital beds on the one hand or financial resources on the other to carry it out in practice. At every level—that of the individual doctor or hospital or that of national expenditure or world organization—a choice has to be made among the sick and the dead. In other words, it is necessary to choose those whose lives are to be and those whose lives are not to be prolonged.

The most reliable workers in the field of medical research and the struggle against death all point to the absurdity of the situation which is rapidly approaching because of the increasing cost of modern therapeutics. In the near future, if this development continues, at least half of the total income of the richest nations will be spent on therapy, unless we decide to give priority to the prevention of disease.[4] Even with regard to his own death, the individual who is dying should not be more isolated from the social reality than he is with regard to everything that has gone to make up his life.

We may therefore conclude that, just as the doctor may have the right or the duty to confine his attention to those patients for whom he is able to do more than simply delay death which is in any case very near, the sick person and those who surround him may also have the right to choose that what may help to delay death is used for what they believe is more beneficial to other people.

II

Almost all the authors who have made a study of this subject are unanimous in concluding that, in present-day medical practice, the dying person and those surrounding him are deprived

[4] For this problem and for the problems raised by present developments in medical science in general, see J. Hamburger, *La puissance et la fragilité* (Paris, 1972) and J. Bernard, *Grandeur et tentations de la médécine* (Paris, 1973).

of almost all responsibility and power of decision-making and that these are now in the hands of the doctor and those in charge of the patient. If nothing more can be done for the dying person by medical means, he and those who surround him find themselves alone, confronting a death and unable to do anything about it. In the past, it was often possible to prepare at home for a "good death", with the help of those who belonged to the family circle. Nowadays, however, the dying person is physically and psychologically removed by purely medical care from his own circle and even from himself. If we are to understand at all whether this is justified, we must understand the reasons for it.

On the one hand, the doctor has a certain knowledge. Certainly in a country like France, in which it has for a long time been normal to withhold from the sick person the gravity of his illness, the doctor knows whether his patient's death is imminent and he of course knows the nature of his illness, its progress and the psychological processes involved. For the sick person and those surrounding him, even the best known illness is often no more than a label or a myth. The possession of this knowledge is, of course, in accordance with the doctor's profession as well as with what the patient and society as a whole expect of him.

On the other hand, in possessing this knowledge, the doctor is also in possession of a certain power. This power is not only technical, but also social and economic. This is also in accordance with his profession and with what the sick person and society expect of him.

When the doctor has to deal with death, this knowledge and this power place him in a paradoxical situation. On the one hand, his task is to prevent patients from dying as well as to guard against and cure illnesses and relieve suffering. His struggle against death cannot be isolated from the general dynamic function of medicine. Any attempt to prevent or to delay death is a logical consequence of any doctor's legitimate attempt to fight for life. The great advances made in the past fifty or so years in medicine have caused a revolution in the minds of those who have been able to benefit from them. In the past, man had only "supernatural" means against fatal illness and death—prayer, magic, superstition—or else very unreliable natural means. Now, however, illness and death are the object of an empirical knowledge and an activity which have clearly been proved effective. Man has power over death and the doctor possesses this power, is responsible for it and is the symbol of it. None the less, death always marks the end of this knowledge and this power, with the result that the doctor regards death as the opposite of medicine. If it is true, as Bichat said at the beginning of the nineteenth century, that "life is the complex of functions which resist death", all men must regard death as the opposite of the desire to live.

Death is, however, also a natural element of life itself and the normal end of an evolutionary cycle which begins with birth, the natural biological consequence of birth. Medicine is a biological science and doctors are therefore best qualified to know that it is natural for biological organisms to die.[5] Not only is death a condition of life itself, in so far as the life of an organism which is complex demands the continuous death of the majority of cells of which it is composed, with the exception of the cells of the nervous system;[6] death also forms part of the very nature of biological life. It is not an accident that happens to life (an accident both in the current and in the Aristotelian sense of the word), but the natural completion of life.

The situation in which medical knowledge and power are placed with regard to death is therefore paradoxical. If life is the total complex of functions which resist death, then it is in the nature of medicine to fight against death. At the same time, however, death is also the logical consequence of the vital process set afoot by conception. Death is therefore the opposite of life. It is not only the enemy of life, however, but also its daughter and mother, because the human organism cannot survive without the death of its cells and its parts.

It is, of course, clear that a distinction should be made be-

[5] See, for example, J. Hamburger, *op. cit.*, pp. 115 ff.
[6] Ought we not to say that the same applies to the social body, the life of which is only possible because of the death of its individual members? How are we to imagine the continued development and survival of the human race if all its individual members had always continued to live?

tween the "natural" death of an old person and death resulting from an "accident" occurring before the termination of the "natural" course of life. This distinction is valuable, but cannot be taken too far, since, although it is undoubtedly natural for a biological organism to end by dying, it is equally natural for the laws governing the organization of living matter to give way to certain fatal risks. Our present knowledge of the physical and chemical laws of living matter leads us to accept the "natural" occurrence of a number of failures at the embryonic, infantile or adult stages of the individual's development because these laws can be combined in such complex ways and because there are so many possible permutations. If we were to suppose that the situation could be different, this would be similar to supposing that matter—expressed in the traditional terms of metaphysics—could be as ontologically simple and perfect as the divine being. Medicine, as a biological science, is therefore placed in the same paradoxical situation here as it is when confronted with "natural" death. On the one hand, it is one of the doctor's tasks to prevent and to cure the consequences or the causes of these risks involved in the combined laws governing living matter and we are all aware of the great advances that have been made in this field. On the other hand, however, these possible fatal risks are part of the very nature of life itself, the life of which the possibility of such risks is not only a property, but also as much a natural consequence of life as death itself. The doctor can therefore do no more with his medical skills to overcome it.

It is therefore easy to understand that doctors are bound to have a paradoxical attitude towards death and that it is within the framework of the conflict in which medical science is situated that our present problem must be considered. At the beginning of the nineteen-fifties, Professor Jean-Robert Debray introduced into French medical terminology the phrase *acharnement thérapeutique* to describe the passion among doctors for using therapeutic processes with effects which are more harmful than those of the illness to be cured or which are useless because cure is impossible or because the hoped-for benefits resulting from such a treatment are much less than the foreseeable disadvantages. Although this whole problem of "therapeutic passion" is involved in many more cases than simply that of the incurably sick,[7] it is certainly true to say that the latter is the most striking and apparently the easiest to solve. In fact, however, it is quite difficult to solve even in the case of incurable sickness. It is, for example, precisely this passion which has made possible certain theoretical and practical discoveries, which have certainly not been of benefit to the sick people who were the objects of this passion, but which have none the less resulted in restoring to life and health many other sick people who had been condemned to death because of the same illness. However spectacular the excesses resulting from the expression of this passion for therapeutics may be in some cases, it would be wrong to explain it simply as the outcome of the doctor's knowledge and immoderate use of power.

In cases such as this, the moralist—whether he is a legislator, a philosopher or a theologian—ought perhaps to be content to say to the doctor what V. Jankélévitch said to him: "Such is the nature of medical casuistry that moral principles are, in most cases, not enough for the doctor to form a decision. It is true to say that morality in its present form can do almost nothing for us."[8]

When the problems of the rights and duties of the dying person, his family circle and the doctor are raised and in view of the fact that, in modern medical practice, the doctor takes the initiative and bears almost all the responsibility, whereas the patient and those surrounding him are passive in this respect, what is most clearly present is not the inner conflict of the doctor, but the possible conflicts between the rights of the dying person and the demands made by the doctor. We must therefore consider the problem from this point of view and reflect about the attitude of the dying person towards his own death.

III

(1) The different sociological and psychological inquiries that have been made about the way in which death is experienced nowadays in Western society have shown that this experience is

[7] See J.-R. Debray, *Le malade et son médecin* (Paris, 1965), pp. 67 ff.
[8] Quoted by J. Hamburger, *op. cit.*, pp. 124-5.

both new and different from in the past. It is new in so far as death is no longer the end of a long preparation for entering the other world, but an immediate experience, centred in the act itself of dying.[9] It is different from the past experience in that very many people now prefer to die suddenly, without any warning and certainly without any preparation. The contrast between death and life is in this case taken to its extreme point, where they are kept strictly separate and not allowed to co-exist. Life must be affected as little as possible by death and death, which is inescapable, must take place as quickly and as efficiently as possible. Whether euthanasia is practised or not, it is a generally held desire that the dying person should be spared a confrontation with death.

Other people, however, believe that, since death belongs to the very essence of man's life, it is a particularly intense time of life which man ought to experience in the most human way possible. The humanization of death is not so much a question of making its approach more gentle and slower as of enabling the dying person and his family circle to turn it into a free action. Some people think that this would justify euthanasia. Whether euthanasia is practised or not, however, it is generally agreed that man dies well if he has a conscious and voluntary attitude towards it. It is, in other words, the importance of death as an anthropological event which gives priority to the rights of the dying person with regard to his own death and not to the rights or duties of the doctor and the nursing staff.

It is, in this context, interesting to note how the problems raised by very different attitudes converge. In France, for instance, an interdisciplinary, non-confessional group of people were commissioned by the Ministry of Public Health to examine the relationships between the doctor and the dying patient. One of their conclusions was that "every man has the right to live his own death. This right must be recognized. It must not be

---

[9] The decreasing influence of Christianity has certainly played a large part in this change. Similar changes of emphasis are, however, known in really authentic Christian faith. In his theology of death, Karl Rahner, for instance, insists on the act of dying itself as a present event without diminishing the importance of the life beyond this life.

imposed, nor must it be monopolized. We have no right to prevent any man from choosing, in so far as it is humanly possible for him to do so, his own death. No person or institution has any legitimate vocation to appropriate another person's death".[10] The theologian Jürgen Moltmann has said that man has a right to his own death just as he has a right to his life, since, as educative human processes, sickness is as important to the personality as health and dying is as important as being born and living.[11]

In view of this, the most important task is to make sure that everything is done to enable the dying person to experience the approach of death consciously and freely and that medicine is used to this end rather than to delay death at all costs. This would, of course, mean that many members of the medical and paramedical professions would have to change their habits of thought and established practices. It would also imply a necessary change in the rules and attitudes of many hospitals and institutions. On the other hand, this problem cannot be reduced to the level of conflict between the rights of the dying person and those of the doctor and nursing staff, nor is it sufficient to call for a change in attitude among doctors and nurses.

(2) From one point of view, the doctor is, after all, symbolic and representative in this case. A deeper and more radical conflict is in fact concealed beneath the conflict that is peculiar to the doctor in charge of the dying patient. We may protest against the great influence exerted by medicine here, but we at the same time ask more of medicine than it is capable of giving. The real problem is that there is a conflict between life and death which is felt less perhaps by the dying person himself than by living people whose will to live is thrown into doubt by every death that they witness. It is also possible that medicine and the biological sciences are problematical not so much because they have an excessive influence on the death of

[10] See the report of a working group under the chairmanship of Dr Claude Veil and published by the French Ministry of Public Health and Social Security: *Les problèmes de la mort* (Paris, 1973), p. 4.

[11] J. Moltmann, "Der Einfluß von Mensch und Gesellschaft auf den biomedizinischen Fortschritt", in R. M. Kunz and H. Fehr, eds., *The Challenge of Life. Biomedical Progress and Human Values* (Basle and Stuttgart, 1972), pp. 328 and 330.

seriously ill patients, but rather because they show that death is part of life. Death indeed forms part of life whether it is the "natural" death of old age or an "accidental" death.

All forms of death were, it was thought for a long time, the result either of a human fault which was consequently punished by the gods[12] or of the activity of evil supernatural or human powers, such as those of a totem, a sorcerer or an enemy. We know now, however, that death is a natural event in life. What we have therefore to consider now is man's attitude towards his own life and death in the light of this fact of "nature". Man is, after all, faced with the contingency of his own life in an entirely new way.

(3) When death is interpreted as a punishment by God or as the result of man's evil doing, this is almost always done in order to deny this contingency of human life, of which death is the sign and the proof. This is so because this interpretation implies that death is not a natural event, but rather the result of an intervention from outside. Man regards death as action performed by gods, devils or his enemies and he does so in order to avoid accepting that it is simply a fact of his own humanity, something that is part of man's nature. Again, if he does not regard it as proceeding from a cause outside himself, he will tend to blame himself for it, thinking that death is the consequence of his own fault and that he has made himself mortal. In this case, too, the deviation is very much the same, in that man can convince himself that, if he had not committed any fault or if he had been delivered from his fault, he would find himself back at what he imagines is his true nature, in other words, a nature to which death was not natural.

This tendency to deny that death is natural to man is very powerful and almost universal. Ethnologists, specialists in comparative religion and psychoanalysts all testify to it. Despite the fact that he is surrounded by evidence of death, man behaves as if he is incapable of recognizing that death is natural. There is no reason therefore for us to be surprised that all that the biological and medical science can teach us about the natural aspect

[12] Quoted by J. H. Baudet and J. M. Palisse, "La vaccination jennerienne", *La Presse Médicale*, 77 (1969), p. 2118.

of death is always being set aside and obscured by what we know from the same science about man's knowledge of and power over sickness, suffering and death.

It is here that the doctor's function as a symbol and as a representative is revealed. He has many good reasons for accepting this function, but he is not the main source of it. His knowledge of and his power over death are considerable and, for this reason, he is in a good position to receive the hopes and demands caused by man's tendency to deny the natural aspect of death. He is also in possession of all the real or mythical privileges of medical science and of its apparently unlimited prospects of further knowledge and its supposedly unbounded power. The dying person and the members of his immediate circle may protest outwardly against the enormous influence of medical science, but inwardly they long and call for it. Medicine thus possesses everything that was in the past sought in supplication to supernatural powers and explained in terms of the supernatural. At the same time, however, the doctor is held responsible for the life and death of his patient—it is normal nowadays to hear it said that things would have been different if only the patient had been better cared for or if the doctor had been more capable or less negligent.

It is, then, true to say that death is nowadays felt to be something that ought not to happen, that ought to be preventable and that may no longer happen one day. Is it at the same time possible that two different truths may perhaps be articulated simultaneously? On the one hand, can we acknowledge the truth that it is part of the greatness of man to be able to struggle more and more against suffering and death? Can we, on the other hand, also admit that it is false greatness on man's part not to accept death as natural to him? As we have seen, however, this is less a medical than a human question. Man in general and every man in particular is involved in it, because it is a question that is raised by the very contingency of his life.

(4) This question cannot be avoided in considering the way in which man ought to experience his death, namely as consciously and as freely as possible. It is undoubtedly part of the dignity of man to be able to prepare himself for death as a supreme

moment of his life. It is impossible to ignore the extent to which death takes place while the dying person is unconscious of it or lacks the will to die. Man should allow his death to enter into the sphere of the consciousness that he has of his own life, but the act of dying cannot always be an object of consciousness for him. It is often impossible for him to be conscious of his dying and this may be for purely psychological reasons. It would in any case be presumptuous to attempt to judge the extent to which a dying person is conscious that he is dying.

Death is, however, a process of disorganization in the biological and psychological functions and of breakdown in the complex whole which forms the human organism. This process begins before death itself in cases of death through sickness. If man is able to prepare himself consciously for death, then death is by definition situated in what lies beyond the consciousness. Man can imagine his death while he is still alive and because he is alive, but he cannot imagine his death when he is dying and because he is dying. There is therefore a final limit to man's possibilities of humanly living his own death if, by "humanly", we mean above all the "will and the power that he exercises when acting".

We are bound to say that it is in accordance with the nature of man's consciousness that his own death should elude him. It is part of man's essential nature that he should not be conscious of the whole of his life at the moment when it reaches its end and its crown, but that his consciousness should rather be dispossessed and loosened of its ties. It may not be wrong therefore to insist on the pre-eminence of consciousness and freedom and on death as an event which man should experience humanly. It is, however, wrong to insist on it in such a way that the fact that a man's own death eludes his consciousness is forgotten would be to fail to recognize what death is naturally for man. This is ultimately a failure to recognize what man himself is and what his life is. This failure of recognition may result in our overrating man's consciousness and freedom, but this will ultimately make no difference apart from the fact that there may also be a failure to appreciate what that consciousness and freedom are and what their contingency means, because they are above all man's consciousness and man's freedom.

(5) There is an element of scandal in the fact that such an important event in his life should elude his consciousness in this way. It is valuable in this instance to go back to the human situation which corresponds to and is at the same time the opposite of death—the beginning of man's life, his conception and earliest development. Like the end of his life, his origin is also something that lies beyond his consciousness. Like the last moments of his life, his first moments do not lend themselves to consciousness and freedom. Both of these two extremes elude man's consciousness, being limits encompassing and defining his life. He cannot have a human relationship with the origin or with the end of his life, nor can he appropriate them. The beginning and the end of his life constitute one of the most striking and at the same time most concealed signs pointing to what his life and its contingency are.

We are therefore bound to ask whether it is not because it is impossible for him to sustain this contingency of his origin and his death that man, in order to be able to deny it, has to regard birth—his origin—and death—his end—as sacred, absolute realities. He is perhaps impelled to base these realities on some necessity, such as gods, devils or nature, precisely because they elude him and because he cannot sustain their contingency. Since his birth and death cannot be the consequence of his own activity, he feels obliged to regard them as resulting from some other superior or inferior will.

At the same time and in the same way, human reproduction and birth on the one hand and death on the other become forbidden territory for him. It is a domain in which he has no right to act or interfere, because it is not his *dominium* or property and he is not *dominus* or lord over it. However justified it may be to restrict man's activity in the domain of his origin and his end, we are none the less bound to ask whether situating his birth and death in forbidden, sacred territory does not in fact result in a concealment and even a denial of man's contingency. In making his origin and his end sacred and in forbidding any activity in his birth and death, man has made himself and his own life absolute—"do not do this and you will be like gods".

We should therefore not be surprised that man's rights regarding human reproduction and birth are being called into question at the same time as his rights with regard to death and that the two most frequently expressed attitudes towards these questions, though apparently contradictory, are in fact similar and closely related. On the one hand, there is the attitude that, because birth and death are absolute values, man must be prevented from controlling them in the same way as he controls his life between conception and death. He has to rely entirely on the absolute principle which directly governs his origin and his end. On the other hand, however, there is the other commonly held view that, because man has the right, as man, to control his life between birth and death, he also has the authority to exercise some control over the two events which are at the very foundation of his life. His consciousness and his freedom as man can, of course, be made so absolute that he will be, as it were, deified. On the other hand, he has no other way of apprehending the truth of his origin and his end than that of discovering what consciousness and freedom mean for him in a mode of being in which consciousness is natural, not an accident.

IV

For the Christian, man's contingent mode of being is the activity of God—the Christian believes that God is the creator and man is the creature. Only God is, in other words, God. In any attempt to define God, we can therefore never have as our object or our result a setting aside of this essential difference which also constitutes man's humanity in the name of God. This difference is not cancelled out by Christ's divine sonship and his resurrection, which transfigure the similarity with God in which creation has placed us originally. Death is intrinsically bound to the nature of living matter in which God originally placed man by creating him. The Church's teaching office has always pointed out that immortality was a praeternatural gift (*praeter naturam*) of grace which was not part of Adam's *naturalis condicio* before his fault.[13]

---

[13] See, for instance, Denzinger-Schönmetzer, 1978 and 2617.

According to Christian teaching, man was not brought back to his original state of wholeness by the resurrection. On the contrary, it brought about a radical change in the order of things—a "new" being and a "new" world. Belief in the resurrection is not a belief in man's return to an immortality which was part of his original nature as created by God, but a belief in the power of the Spirit, who brought Jesus back from death to life, to change the old order of things and make all things new. That is why, like the cross, the resurrection is also foolishness to some and a scandal to others. Sharing in the death and resurrection of Jesus Christ makes us, according to St Paul (Rom. 6. 13) "men who have been brought from death to life" and not living men who do not have to die and for whom death is not natural.

It would seem therefore that to present death as an accident which is not in accordance with man's nature is not the best way of doing justice to faith in the creation of man and the resurrection. On the contrary, this way of viewing man's death would seem to exalt God, but it is at the same time a false exaltation of man, failing to recognize what man really is in God's creation and even failing to recognize what the Spirit of God is in bringing believers back from death to life. If this is in fact so, Christians have above all to ask what it is that leads them so often to deny, in the name of their faith, the natural aspect of death. An honest answer to this question might also lead them to a fresh assessment of their theological, liturgical and pastoral understanding of death. It is just as important for Christians to do this as it is for them—and doctors and their colleagues—to reflect about the meaning of death today for medical science and modern society. It is undoubtedly their first task.

Translated by David Smith

Gisbert Greshake

Towards a Theology of Dying

OVER the past two decades, many books and articles have been written on a "theology of death".[1] Under the influence of existentialism, these have highlighted our awareness of the finite nature of man in death and have shown death to be a privileged moment of human freedom and a point of Christian hope. But little attention has been given, in this theological perspective, to the actual dying human. Interest has been focused on death, not dying, on the final moment, not on the long drawn out process leading immediately up to the end itself. Admittedly death and dying are inseparably linked with each other, and to this extent the various available proposals for a theology of death also provide noteworthy indications for a theology of dying. But little theological consideration is yet given to dying itself, and a theology of dying remains an important desideratum of further theological work, especially today when numerous disciplines in the human sciences are showing their concern for the dying.

What is expounded in what follows is intended to offer only a small contribution to a theology of dying. Its aim is three-fold. Firstly, we shall consider what has come to be known as the hypothesis of a final decision, something that has been prominent in Catholic theology over the last few years. Secondly,

[1] See especially: Karl Rahner, *On the Theology of Death* (Freiburg and London, 1961); R. Troisfontaine, *I Do Not Die* ... (New York, 1963); Ladislaus Boros, *The Moment of Truth* (London, 1965); E. Jüngel, *Tod* (Stuttgart, 1971).

we shall try to outline the biblical data relating to the subject of dying and to work out their systematic content. Thirdly, we shall use this as the basis for making some connections with present-day concern for the dying.

I. Is Dying Man's Fully Personal, Freest Action?

Of recent years dying has only directly been the object of theological reflection within the context of the hypothesis of a final decision. However differently this may have been presented in detail by the many theologians and philosophers who have dealt with it,[2] nearly all of them are agreed on the following three points in connection with the concept of "transcendental subjectivity", a concept coloured by existentialism.

1. The moment of death is admittedly quite beyond empirical observation. But it is possible to ascertain what happens in this action on the boundary of life by extrapolating from the achievement of the whole of life. It is a question as it were of considering the limit towards which the graph of someone's life tends without ever actually reaching it. If, in the fulfilment of his life, man is always matter *and* spirit, necessity *and* freedom, then dying must contain this real dialectic. This means that death may be not only a destructive event from outside, a biological occurrence or an incalculable rupture, but also "an active consummation from within brought about by the person himself, ... a growing up, the result of what man has made of himself during this life, the achievementt of total self-possession".[3] What constitutes the whole of human life—the interaction of the impotence of suffering and the freedom of action, of being dominated by others and autonomy—therefore reaches its highest point in death. At the point where in death man suffers total external domination over himself, he is asked to make the final and supreme active expression of his freedom.

---

[2] The most important proponents of this theory are: H. E. Hengstenberg, *Einsamkeit und Tod* (Regensburg, 1938); P. Glorieux, "In hora mortis", in *Mélanges. Sc. Rel.*, 6 (1949), pp. 185–216; R. W. Gleason, "Toward a Theology of Death," in *Thought (Fordham University Quarterly)* 23 (1957) pp. 39–68; Rahner, Troisfontaine, Boros, *op. cit.;* Josef Pieper, *Death and Immortality* (London 1969).

[3] Rahner, *op. cit.* p. 39.

In this way, he either accepts death as a fulfilment and enters the mystery of God or he closes himself in on himself in a final protest. Death is therefore "the highest moral act, whereby man freely consummates his whole existence".[4] It is, as L. Boros so clearly saw,[5] the actual moment of becoming human: "Death gives man the opportunity of posing his first completely personal act; death is, therefore, by reason of its very being, the moment above all others for the awakening of consciousness, for freedom, for the encounter with God, for the final decision about his eternal destiny."

2. The act of death is completely personal and absolutely free because it takes place at the moment of separation of body and soul. The spirit, liberated from the fetters of time and matter, is thus made entirely itself "in a total awareness and presence of being".[6]

3. This act of decision is placed at the moment of death. The objection cannot therefore be made to a theology of dying that it does not correspond to the concrete experience of dying, since man is often unconscious or impotent at death or finds that death has suddenly come on him unawares, so that the possibility of a free decision does not exist. This objection is answered by recourse to the metaphysical concept of the moment of death, which lacks extension and is fundamentally incapable of observation and verification, and which is not identical with the lapse of time involved in the process of dying. In this connection reference is also made to contemporary medicine's recognition that death takes place gradually, so that death in the final and conclusive sense is not identical with the organic process of dying.[7]

---

[4] *Ibid.*, p. 103.   [5] *Op. cit.* p. 9.

[6] Boros, *op. cit.*, p. 7. See also Troisfontaine, *op. cit.* (German edition) pp. 120, 133; P. Schoonenberg, "Und das Leben der zukünftigen Welt", in H. H. Berger and others, *Leben nach dem Tode* (Cologne, n.d.), pp. 98 f.

[7] The following additional arguments in favour of the hypothesis are considered noteworthy by Boros, Troisfontaine and Schoonenberg: (1) It is only if such a fully personal final decision is made that human life comes to true perfection of itself; (2) only this hypothesis makes it possible to understand that in death the state of pilgrimage reaches its completion, and indeed in the sense that the basic direction of human freedom, as it ensues in the final decision, is irrevocable, even in the encounter with God after death; (3) this theory opens up the possibility in death of a

Yet, however impressive this theology of dying, as a completely personal and free decision on man's part, may be and however fruitfully it can be applied to solve other theological problems, there are still several objections that can be raised against it.

1. The whole force of the theological theory of the final decision rests on the meaning of a transempirical event that fundamentally escapes experience and verification. What is objectionable about it is not only that it thereby is moved to an area of uncertainty and continuous indeterminability but that it also leaves out of consideration and depreciates the concrete fact of dying in all its different forms. In this way this theological theory does not affect the person who is dying at all and cannot therefore be of any real assistance either to him or to those who are looking after him.

2. The assertion of the dialectical unity of passive suffering and free action in the moment of death cannot simply be supported with a reference to the unity of freedom and necessity, of activity and passivity, that constitutes and characterizes the whole of human life. For, as E. Jüngel[8] has rightly observed: "There is a passivity without which man would not be human. This includes the fact of being born ... and it includes the fact of dying." And who can say whether dying does not reduce us to a passivity like that of birth?

3. The theory implies that at the moment of death—and therefore "before" the encounter with God—life reaches its inner consummation and finds its identity.[9] It will be shown later that this one-dimensional acceptance of the biblical findings is not completely correct—quite apart from the way in which the undialectical assertion of the meaning of death, in contrast to

---

personal decision of faith in the case of young children, the mentally afflicted, and the unevangelized.

[8] *Op. cit.*, p. 116.

[9] J. Pieper has gone so far as to write, *op. cit.*, p. 88, that death "is always an act completing existence from within, ... a real bringing to an end, rounding out of the whole of life. ... In saying this we are above all voicing the consoling and immediately persuasive idea that strictly speaking there can be no such thing as an untimely or premature death. Rather, a man always dies 'at the end of his life', in a far more exact sense than we usually realize."

its being experienced as nonsensical and devoid of meaning, must necessarily come under the suspicion of ideology.

4. In this theory too much weight is put on the moment of death as the one and only completely personal and free decision, so that it is made the privileged point of human existence. But this leads to a devaluation of the significance of concrete human life (including dying as the concluding phase of life) and an inversion of the precedence of life over death as recognized by human experience and emphasized in the Bible.[10]

However questionable the theological hypothesis of the final decision may be, it has at the same time the merit of having directed attention to some aspects both of methodology and of content that retain their validity even independently of a hypothetical final decision at the moment of death. What is more, their real significance only appears if they are linked not with the transempirical moment of death, but with the actual process of dying. In fact it is dying itself and not just the hypothetical moment of transition that is an exceptional situation of decision which shows the concentration and sharpening of what has already always existed in the fulfilment of human life. For this reason the sense, meaning and reality of dying cannot be considered independently of the experience of life but can only be regarded as its extreme limiting factor. To speak of dying one has to speak of living. This methodological principle is correctly referred to by the hypothesis of the final decision. And this too is the procedure of Scripture. We must now apply ourselves to its basic statements on the subject of dying, as these

---

[10] Admittedly all the authors see the final decision in connection with the decisions made during life. In their view, however, something qualitatively new is involved in the final decision, in view of its fully personal nature, its totality, and its absolute freedom, with the result that we have basically to deal with a correction of the previous decisions made during life. But the consequent overburdening of the final decision comes into conflict with the dogma of death as the conclusion of man's state of pilgrimage. For, since the advocates of the theory have to place this final act of freedom at the *moment of transition*, since it is only then that man is freed from the limiting conditions of materiality and fragmentality, the final decision already falls outside the human condition, even though it is postulated that it still belongs to the situation of the state of pilgrimage. The artificial nature of the hypothesis is shown precisely in the ontological description of the situation of transition.

have been set out by recent exegesis. If theology does not want to run wild among unverifiable speculations, it must take its standard from Scripture. What follows presents the complex biblical findings in a systematic form.

II. The Ambiguous Meaning of Dying in Scripture

"All that a man has he will give for his life" (Job 2. 4)—this sentence expresses the Old Testament assessment of life as the highest good.[11] But in the Old Testament life does not mean just bare existence. Life is rather only to be found where it is realized in community with other men, in security, health, peace, fortune and happiness. This kind of fulfilled life is God's gift over which man has no control and which is given to man by God for his blessing and salvation. Moreover, since Yahweh is the source of life (Ps. 36. 9), the gift of life is not something that can be separated from the giver. Hence life essentially means standing in a certain relationship to God. But life is not only a gift—it also imposes a duty. Man receives it to embody it in the service of God and according to God's instructions. Hence we frequently find in the Old Testament the promise of life linked with the proclamation of the commandments, and this connection is something that we should at once "claim generally as a constitutive element of faith in Yahweh".[12]

So life as a gift and as a duty is, in its origin and its meaning, removed from man's control and leads him towards his relationship to God. It is never a possession which he can control. He only obtains life while he endeavours continually to win it anew from God. The fact that life is limited in time is in the earlier Old Testament literature accepted almost without question.[13] It is no use struggling against it—man is like grass that withers (Isa. 40. 6–7). "We must all die, we are like water spilt on the ground, which cannot be gathered up again" (2 Sam. 14. 14). But

[11] For what follows see G. Greshake, *Auferstehung der Toten* (Essen, 1969), pp. 175 ff., where the most important literature is also cited.

[12] G. von Rad, " 'Gerechtigkeit' und 'Leben' in den Psalmen", in *Festschrift A. Bertholet*, ed. W. Baumgartner and others (Tübingen, 1950), p. 427.

[13] The reasons for this are brought together in Greshake, *op. cit.,* pp. 186 ff.

death is not for this reason "the last enemy". Rather in dying the breath of life that Yahweh has destined for man ceases. Thus death as the frontier of life, which is the gift of Yahweh, becomes involved in man's relationship to God: it is under the dominion of God (cf. Deut. 32. 39).

Because this limitation is an integral part of life, the truth of God's salvation has to be shown here and now within the boundaries marked out for life by birth and death. And the Old Testament's message about this is that the person to whom God gives himself in friendship and who complies with God's commandments is given by Yahweh a long and fortunate life for which dying does not mean just a dismal conclusion but a consummation, not a fear-laden crisis but a peaceful fulfilment. Abraham is thus promised: "You shall go to your fathers in peace; you shall be buried in a good old age" (Gen. 15. 15). And the promise is thus fulfilled: "Abraham breathed his last and died in a good old age, an old man and full of years" (Gen. 25. 8). "Full of years" and "in a ripe old age" is how those die who are blessed by God (cf. Gen. 35. 29, Judges 8. 32, Job 42. 17, 1 Chr. 23. 1, 29. 28, 2 Chr. 24. 15). In this way dying can be the fortunate fulfilment of human life and death the reward of an age rich in blessings. "You shall come to your grave in ripe old age, as a shock of grain comes up to the threshing floor in its season" (Job 5. 26).

If there are also passages in the Old Testament which express man's bitterness about the necessity of dying and which reach their climax in the statement that the dead are "those whom thou (Yahweh) dost remember no more" (Ps. 88. 5), death is in general accepted as the natural boundary of life. Since the finiteness of life comes from God, the power of death is the power of Yahweh. At the boundary of life stands the living God and nothing else. It is from this belief that there develops at a relatively late stage, though with great urgency, the hope in the overcoming of death through God's power of resurrection.

Dying as the peaceful fulfilment of life is only one aspect of the Old Testament experience of faith. The Old Testament also recognizes the necessity of dying before life has been fulfilled and can reach its consummation. There is sudden, premature, "evil" death, "death in the midst of one's days", which already

sends its harbingers among men. Sickness, poverty, need, loneliness, despair are realities of death that already affect life,
diminish it in its positive qualities and make it come to an end
before its time. This kind of dying is very closely connected
with sin. For the sinner wants to gain life from his own resources
without God and against God. But precisely because of this,
separated from the source of his life, he loses life (in its fullness)
—he must die.

It is only through a radical turning towards God that he will
be freed from the power of "evil death"—the just man "avoids
the snares of death" (Prov. 14. 27). This and similar sayings do
not indicate an overcoming of the boundary of death but rather
a liberation from the sphere of death's power that is realized
here and now in the sinner, where death reduces the fullness of
(earthly) life to nothing and brings it to a premature conclusion.
Thus the just man lives and the sinner dies. But this connection
between what one does and one's destiny necessarily faces a
profound crisis, since it is clear that "evil death" affects not
only the life of the sinner, but also that of the just man and
that the sinner, whose aim is to live for himself alone, often
enjoys a better "life" than the just man, who for his part often
experiences the affliction of this menacing aspect of death to a
greater extent in his "life". At the same time, it also shows that
the image of dying as a natural consummation and peaceful
fulfilment of life, as represented in the death of the just in the
Old Testament, is indeed a possibility but not necessarily a fact.
This is the way one *could* die, it *would be good* to die this way,
but in fact things are often different. In fact, man dies although
he has not reached fulfilment, he dies too young or he dies
although he is not really ready for death. Hence dying is in fact
a curse for the just and the unjust alike, since both are affected
by the same fate of having to die without being able to reach
fulfilment in death.

The Old Testament, in its Yahwistic sections above all, therefore proclaims in a germinal form what is fully developed in
the New, the idea that dying cannot be "natural" and thus
cannot be willed by God. Death is, in other words, "the wages
of sin" and shows itself in its actual form as a curse and affliction.
It is seen as the consequence of the fact that man does not

understand his life as a gift of God implying a duty towards
God and does not receive it from God in confidence and thanks,
but that he lives it without God and wants to bring it to fulfilment without God. In this case however dying becomes the
extreme proof of the impotence of a life that seeks to define
itself in its own terms. This however raises afresh the question
as to how man can fulfil his life when he has to die too young
and what the death of the just man really means. The Old
Testament is only able to nibble at the edges of a solution to
these problems, inasmuch as it directs one's hope towards
resurrection and gives the just man's suffering and dying the
power of reconciliation and salvation. In this way, dying in the
Old Testament shows a characteristic ambiguity. On the one
hand, it is a peaceful fulfilment of oneself and, on the other,
a nonsensical breaking off of life.

It is the second line which is almost exclusively pursued by
the New Testament. In Paul's theology death is precisely the
"definition of man under the power of sin".[14] The sinner refuses
to receive his life as a gift of God implying a duty towards God,
he wants to have his own "life". But inasmuch as he lives
for himself alone (cf. 2 Cor. 5. 15) he is in fact abandoned to
himself and to his own capabilities in which he intends to have
life. But these potentialities—prosperity, freedom, the future—
turn out in their conclusion to be null and void. The inevitability of death stamps every would-be autonomous life as death,
every salvation as its reverse, every freedom as entanglement
in one's own powerlessness. What is involved in the sinner's
life becomes almost palpable in his dying—a life that imagines
it can exercise control over itself runs away into emptiness and
nothing.

Jesus' proclamation of God's reign is the summons of life to
those whose lives are lacking. Man must open himself to God
and to God's claim on him. He must break out of the suffocating
narrowness of his own self and accept life as a gift from God
imposing a duty towards God. He must try continually to surrender his life in service to God and his brothers. It is only the
man who does this who will gain life now and in the future

---

[14] On this see G. Schunack, *Das hermeneutische Problem des Todes*
(Tübingen, 1967); Greshake, *op. cit.*, pp. 246 ff.

(cf. Mark 8: 34 ff., 10. 29 ff. and parallel passages). But who-ever ignores the summons of life already belongs among the dead (cf. Luke 9. 60) and whoever from now on lives for himself alone and is anxious about his own possessions and advantage must come to realize, at the latest at his hour of death, that his life has had no foundation or stability (cf. Luke 12. 15 ff.). In this way the New Testament does not see in dying the natural occurrence of the completion of life but rather points to death as the power of sin that turns dying into a nonsensical breaking off.

It is this dismal experience of dying that Jesus takes upon him-self. True, it cannot clearly be discerned historically what under-standing the earthly Jesus had of his death and in what attitude and state of mind he died. But it is likely that Jesus experienced his dying as a dark and bitter breaking off of his life. He did not die the "good death" of the just men of the Old Testament or the harmonious death of the hero such as Plato describes in the example of Socrates. He died the death of the sinner, and the possibility cannot be excluded that he died in bitter despair. He whose life was defined and marked out by the closeness of God, who in an unprecedented way had brought close to men God's reign with its promise of life, was rejected, betrayed, left in the lurch by his own, with his work left unfinished, with his message apparently reduced to absurdity.

He died alone, the painful death of a condemned criminal on the cross. His last cry, which the accounts are agreed in reporting (cf. Mark 15. 34–37, Heb. 5. 7), could well have arisen from despair at this divine absurdity.[15] Yet, even if the last words of Jesus as they have come down to us are later interpretations, they show clearly that Jesus did not die "cursing against God, but rather in a despairing flight towards God".[16] Psalm 22, which he was, according to Mark 15. 34, uttering at his death, claims God's covenant loyalty towards man for God's sake. "The emphasis is on the cry 'My God' ... The Son thus still clings to faith at a time when faith seems to have become mean-

[15] Jüngel, op. cit., p. 134.
[16] A. Strobel, Kerygma und Apokalyptik (Göttingen, 1967), p. 144.

ingless and earthly reality proclaims God's absence".[17] Since
Jesus in this way dies the nonsensical death of the sinner in a
final "despairing trust" in God, since Jesus surrenders himself
to the abyss of death in the hope of finding God even there,
since in the experience of the boundary of death the Son clings
firmly to his Father as the boundless source of life, God responds
with the proof of his loyalty. God awakens him to new life.
He gives a new identity and a new relationship, since in death
all identity and all relationships are broken. What is more, God
identifies himself with the Jesus who suffered and died for us,
so that his dying and with it the dying of all of us finds the
point of entry to the life of God. Through Jesus' dying the
world's history of suffering and death is taken up into the
history of God. For this reason all dying is freed from final
darkness and from the lack of any way out, it is redeemed from
the curse of merely placing the final seal on the sinner's hopeless
and meaningless selfish existence. Jesus' death makes it possible
for our dying to be the consummation of life in God.

Of course, for Christ's disciples—and here we take up again
one of the insights of the theological hypothesis of the final
decision—dying still remains the final and most difficult con-
firmation and realization of what living in the imitation of
Christ already demands, that is not to cling on to one's self and
one's life but to surrender it in order to gain it afresh from God.

Thus at the centre of carrying out the imitation and following
of Christ there stands the genuine reality of dying as an inner
factor of true life. This is expressed by the New Testament statements that describe the life of the Christian as dying with Christ.
This dying with Christ is not anything negative but rather a
liberation from a life that only seeks itself and for that reason is
lacking and is really "death". The person who dies with Christ
receives his life again as God's gift that is conveyed to him as
imposing its own duty and thereby gains a share in the life that
persists and is real. This dying and rising again with Christ
constitutes the Christian life from the time of baptism and the
decision of faith onwards (cf. Rom. 6. 2 ff., John 5. 24). Paul
makes this clear to his congregations above all by the example

[17] E. Käsemann, "Die Gegenwart des Gekreuzigten", in *Christus unter
uns* (Stuttgart and Berlin, 1967), pp. 6, 9.

of his own person: "I die every day" (1 Cor. 15. 31, and see also 2 Cor. 4. 7 ff., Gal. 6. 17, Rom. 8. 36). "We are treated . . . as dying, and behold we live" (2 Cor. 6. 9). The hard and dangerous work of the missionary, the daily business of wearing oneself out in the service of the Christian communities and love of the brethren are ways of dying and of surrendering life. It is in turning away from a life which wants to cling firmly to itself, but which in reality is only "death", and in communion with Christ and the relationship to God that is mediated by him that death is overcome (cf. John 11. 25 ff.). He who loves has already "passed out of death into life" (1 John 3. 14).[18]

In this perspective even the biological process of dying becomes relative. "If we live, we live to the Lord, and if we die, we die to the Lord; so then, whether we live or whether we die, we are the Lord's" (Rom. 14. 8). "Neither death nor life . . . will be able to separate us from the love of God" (Rom. 8. 38–9). "For me to live is Christ and to die is gain" (Phil. 1. 21, cf. 1 Cor. 3. 21–3).

Of course, as an immediate and unavoidable confrontation with death, the biological process of dying remains still a situation of radical decision where man is asked how he has understood himself and his life and now—in retrospect—wishes to understand it. The time immediately before the end, the process of dying, provides a last possible way for man, who is essentially free, to determine the pattern of his life. Moreover, since during life dying with Christ always takes place in a fragmentary form, the final process of dying not only bears the character of the beatific consummation of oneself, but also brings with it the final bitter experience of the nothingness of life. Hence Paul can interpret dying completely within the context of the Jewish theology of suffering as punishment and possibility for sin (cf. 1 Cor. 11. 32, 5. 5).

Yet it remains true that the Christian is fundamentally liberated from the kind of dying that as the final consequence of sin is merely meaningless and absurd. In undergoing death as the

[18] Thus in love both dying and the gaining of true life are anticipated. There are frequent references to this in the literature. Cf., e.g., Boros, *op. cit.,* pp. 56–7; F. Ulrich, *Leben in der Einheit von Leben und Tod* (Frankfurt, 1973).

biological frontier of life he is "passive in another way than in undergoing death that has been incurred as a curse in consequence of his own actions. In this kind of death, the kind that is experienced as a curse, man is the subject of an activity that he must then undergo passively. But the conclusion of life that is freed from death as a curse is undergone by man in a passivity that is dependent on the activity of the creator. This kind of passivity cannot be an evil."[19]

III. Consequences for the Practical Expression of Christianity

If anything like a single thread runs through the various biblical statements about dying, it is that speaking about dying is very closely linked with speaking about life. Dying is not the goal and horizon of the meaning of life so that life becomes devalued to a preparation for death (*ars moriendi*), but rather the reverse—life which is all-embracing includes death as an inner factor in itself. Hence Christian faith invites the dying person to look upon life. But this look can be very different in keeping with the ambiguous meaning of death as the consummation of human life in God or as the final seal of impotence on the life that seeks itself alone. The theological consequences for the care of those who are dying are therefore also different.

1. *Dying as a Consummation of Life*

A long, full life which is completed in a "natural" death from old age (which up to now has only occurred in a ratio of 1 to 100,000) and which finds a peaceful death in God is clearly, according to Scripture, part of the full human existence originally willed by God. For this reason, Christian faith, which is aware of the redemption through Jesus Christ of the *whole* man, including his dying, must to an especial degree exert itself to obtain the social and individual conditions in which the possibility of living and dying in this way is made easier and in which the assistance and the conditions that the dying man needs to this end are made available.[20] Assistance is both inward

[19] Jüngel, *op. cit.,* pp. 115 f.
[20] Here consequently the demands of Christian faith meet the non-

or spiritual and outward or physical. By assistance of the more physical kind is meant not only the medical care that is right for the dying person but above all the creation of conditions that correspond to the personal dignity of man in the last stages of his life. The fact that many people die in physical isolation, either in intensive care units separated from personal contact with their fellow patients, nurses and doctors by a wilderness of technical apparatus and instruments, or in side-rooms in hospitals that increasingly see themselves as "service stations for health and optimal biotechnical care",[21] cannot by any means be reconciled with the dignity of the dying person, since man "comes to his grave in ripe old age, as a shock of grain comes up to the threshing floor in its season" (Job 5. 26).

What is already possible today and could well be further expanded in the future, the maintenance of purely vegetative existence by means of complicated apparatus, brings with it at the very least the danger of reducing the dying person to an object and of wringing a minimal biological existence from death not so much for the sake of the dying person as for the sake of medical egoism and self-assertion. It is possible in this way to celebrate the victory of man's technical ability, but it hardly does justice to the situation of dying as the final personal stage of maturity in someone's life. Just as human life ought not to be cut short and limited by any external agency, since it is only in God that it has its limits, so ought it not to be maintained at a sub-personal level, that is only by the technical maintenance of certain life-functions without any prospect of further personal life. Part of the doctor's art is to help man towards a peaceful consummation of life.

Besides these outward or physical ways of helping the dying there are others of a more inward or spiritual kind. If dying is the consummation of life and entry into the life of God, then,

---

Christian aims and concepts of a "natural death". This "demands a society in which this kind of natural death is the rule or at the least can become the rule. It must be possible for everyone to die at the time when his powers and faculties have reached their end, to live out to the limit of his biological life-forces without violence or disease or premature death": W. Fuchs, *Todesbilder in der modernen Gesellschaft* (Frankfurt, 1973), p. 72.

[21] K.-H. Bloching, *Tod* (Mainz, 1973), p. 27.

however paradoxical it may sound, the dying person must be strengthened in what he wants of life, in his hope and love for life. It is only if life has meaning that death has too, and it is precisely this truth that has to be verified in the final stage of life. This theological demand falls in with the findings of the secular sciences which indicate that in general dying people have the desire to remain in contact with everyday life and want time to live, be it ever so short. It is precisely those who love life for whom death loses some of its terror.[22] St Francis of Assisi's Canticle of the Sun, a hymn of praise to life written on his deathbed, can provide an eloquent example of this.

From the point of view of Christian faith too, it is therefore important to pay attention to and indeed to ensure that the dying person is concerned about his relatives, that as opportunity offers he still deals with the various practical affairs of everyday life, that he even still goes on making long-cherished plans for the future. All this gives the dying person the feeling of fulfilling his life. And in this, hope in the eternal life to come can free him from egoistical concern about his own living and dying: it can open the dying person to a selfless final concern for the life of others and to a readiness consciously and willingly to make room for the coming generation. Christian care for the dying will try to support and encourage all these "little hopes" that the dying person shows. For it is only the person who entertains "little" and "penultimate" hopes and who sees in these God's gift and promise of life who can also cherish the "great" hope in a never-ending future to his life, a hope that is in fact actually promised and sketched out in advance in these little hopes.[23] Indeed, it is only when hope is directed towards the power of God that arouses life that dying can be experienced as the consummation of life in its ultimate and complete sense. This power of God is the only point of reference which

---

[22] "I have often noted that men who live intensely and know why they are alive are much more serene in old age and death. They accept the latter as the normal term of their maturation and achievements—and this quite independently of their belief in personal survival": Ignace Lepp, *Death and its Mysteries* (London, 1969), p. 140.

[23] For this terminology distinguishing between "great" and "little" and "final" and "penultimate" hopes cf. Karl Barth, *Kirchliche Dogmatik* IV: 1, pp. 131 f., and Greshake, *op. cit.*, pp. 85 f.

can still give identity, meaning and a future to the life that is expiring.

It is here that Christian concern for the dying is distinguished from all one-dimensional attempts to try to encounter death meaningfully as the natural end. Christian hope is imparted to the dying person not only verbally but above all by the personal attitude of those around the deathbed, an attitude that does not suppress the imminence of death, and by indications of love and concern. It is in the apparently pointless love that is shown to the dying person up to the end through the presence of others and their touching and caressing him that it is most convincingly brought home to him that the human community of love is not destroyed even by death. "To love someone means to say: you will not die."[24] The same function is performed by the liturgy of the dying. The very presence of the priest can be a silent sign of that hope that still remains steadfast when everything else is destroyed. In the liturgy of the dying, the Church accompanies the dying person to the boundary and as it were hands him over to God and the heavenly "community of the saints". Thus it is a sign of the hope that dying does not destroy the community of love.

2. Dying as the Experience of Absurdity and Impotence

Up till now we have only looked at the consequences that arise from considering only one aspect of the ambiguous nature of dying. Everything that has been said would remain one-sided and therefore false if we were not to consider that the redemption of the process of dying through Jesus Christ has, like all redemption, only been partially realized and still awaits its completion. Even if the Christian has put behind him death in its sense of the "consequence of sin" and dying as the final mark of a nonsensical life that shuts out God and his claims and builds on itself alone and even if he should already in the course of his life have continually realized dying as an element of true living, yet all this can only be done in a fragmentary way. Hence even for the redeemed dying is experienced not simply as the natural consummation of his life but is always

[24] G. Marcel, *Das Geheimnis des Seins* (Vienna, 1952), p. 472.

also experienced as the pressing in of non-existence, as the depths of misery and alarm.[25] Because "dying with Christ" is always something that can only take place in a fragmentary way, because man has "died" too little in his life, dying is for this reason ultimately not only a consummation but at the same time a bitter and miserable end.

One must first gradually learn, with difficulty, to renounce the life that earlier one did not want to give up. Involved in alarm at dying is not only fear of what is to come but above all the negative experience of what is past. "The emptiness of the experience of this life arouses fear of the emptiness of the next world."[26] If the person concerned should for the most part have expressed himself during his life in possessing, doing and consuming things, then he "must" resist dying, he must suppress and deny death.[27] It is therefore clear that it is not so much death as the life that lies behind one and that is now about to reach its conclusion that has to be overcome and mastered. Seen in this way, dying is the moment of truth, the various phases of which, from refusal to peaceful readiness, have been impressively described by E. Kübler-Ross.[28] It is the latest moment for accepting that life does not belong to one and that it cannot bring about its own consummation and perfection by means of however extended a prolongation in time. In this way dying gives man his last chance to break out of himself, to leave his life, in which he formerly did not want to die with Christ, and to go forward towards God's future. This too is shown by the evidence of dying people who have encountered a bound-

[25] The problem is not solved by the Marxist and neopositivist thesis of death as a natural end that can be experienced in a society free from repression through the acceptance of this state of affairs. On this see Fuchs, *op. cit.*, p. 219. Fear of dying goes deeper than social conditions or a failure to make explicit enlightenment on death. Minimizing this fear will lead to further repression of the idea of death and the creation of numerous neuroses if the real reason for this fear is not made specific. It is clear that when faced with death a purely emancipatory conception of man collapses and that at this point is shown the truth of life as God's absolute gift. On this complex of problems see G. Scherer, *Der Tod als Frage der Freiheit* (Essen, 1971).

[26] R. Leuenberger, *Der Tod* (Zürich, 1971), p. 127.

[27] Cf. D. Sölle, "Der Tod in der Mitte des Lebens" (speech at the Evangelical Kirchentag 1973), in *Herder-Korrespondenz* 27 (1973), p. 412.

[28] Elisabeth Kübler-Ross, *On Death and Dying* (New York, 1969).

lessly expanding area of inner freedom precisely in confronting death.[29]

In this context we can see as not only naturally understandable but also as extremely meaningful from the theological point of view the effort many dying people make to put their affairs in order, to make some kind of final sense of their life, to settle conflicts that are still going on, to make peace, to forgive wrongs, to clear up anything in a muddle. Acceptance of dying as the consummation of one's life in God—all that we have been considering in the previous section—presupposes acceptance of one's previous life. And because this is an area where we are never totally successful on our own account, because our life has always been to some extent a life of self-assertion and selfish rigidity, man needs God's forgiveness when he dies. He needs God's acceptance of his life and the assurance that "God writes straight with crooked lines". This too is a further important aspect of the liturgy of the dying—it assures the dying person of the forgiving presence of Christ and God's unconditional acceptance.

3. *Death without "Dying"*

Just as contemporary life leaves many people no time for living, so death leaves many no time for dying.[30] There are the countless victims of traffic accidents, the victims of war and violence, the massacres that ignore the individual, the diseases that bring death suddenly without any previous warning. In all these cases death cannot be preceded by a process of dying in the sense of achieving an inner maturity. Just as in the Old Testament the really alarming aspect of death was when it was sudden and premature, so today the situation is the same only more so. Jesus' dying is an answer to the death of the many who die without "dying". Jesus died without consolation or company, without hearing words of love and hope, without being able to complete his life and work as they needed to be completed. In taking over this nonsensical and absurd death as his own and opening up to it the new future of the resurrection, God showed that he is close to the dying of all those who with-

[29] On this see Pieper, *op. cit.*, p. 93.
[30] Cf. Leuenberger, *op. cit.*, p. 125.

out time for maturity and completion die a banal, accidental and senseless sudden death. Thus Jesus' death gives hope to this kind of death, and hope is the real message that Christian faith has to give with regard to death and dying.

Translated by Robert Nowell

Hubert Lepargneur

The Church's Critical Function regarding Death as Ordered by Society

WEEK by week the mass media present us with types of deadly violence that society has not only been unable to avoid but has even provoked and alongside these news items statements are made by Church leaders condemning this violence and calling for peace. Is the juxtaposition of these two aspects of the situation enough to quieten our consciences as men and as Christians? Is the exacerbation of violence in the world inevitable, the price of growth in love on the part of a few, or is it the product of some technical failure that progress will finally eliminate?

The front page of the newspapers seems to run a competition in effectiveness between earthquakes, wars, drownings, murders, volcanic eruptions, epidemics, aeroplane accidents, declarations of peace and outbreaks of armed conflict. The cultural operation fertilizes the womb of nature for life and for death, but the specific task of society is to transform human destiny into history. Only Christ conquers death, but we all have the task of humanizing life when it reaches its end. Only Christ's cross gives a positive meaning to death, but the task of humanization should make death less absurd, and useless violence less frequent. The Church nowadays has the task of humanizing death. But how —without playing at gods, without being pharisaical, or unrealistic—can the Church fulfil this task today?

It is true that life is bound up with risk and that risk involves death. Thus death, even when violent, is not the infallible criterion by which the validity of a planned or tolerated operation can be judged. The conditions must be closely examined in each case. What risks, for example, are legitimate? For what vital activities and what aspects of progress are risks to be taken? What risks are too often fatal and should be controlled by urgent and humane technical progress? It is not, for instance, admissible for this or that building project to cost the life of one workman each month or each week. Unquestionably we must slow down the speed with which we want to enter the future, build the town with stones, increase production, catch up with technological delays or outstrip competing powers. And unquestionably the Church should say all this.

I. THE DATA AND TRADITIONAL MORALITY

1. *Facts and Situations: the Society that Protects also Kills*

The secular city likes to boast of the freedom it allows, the consumer goods it promotes, and the amusements it provides. It hides its dead, its suicides, its funerals and its graveyards. It shamelessly crams its entertainments with scenes of violence as if it did not know that violence leads to death. The people enjoy that. The taste for violence is well rooted in human beings. Its results are war, riots, capital punishment, murders, suicides, accidents on building sites or at work in general, road deaths[1] and the cost in human lives accepted or tolerated by governments. None of this is excluded from our subject-matter.

Violence is growing in the modern world. Though it takes different forms, it always arises from a basis of irrationality, and far from having been tamed by technical and scientific achievements, it has been positively exacerbated by the building of the secular city whose apparent rationality ill conceals all its contradictions and tensions. On the one hand the secular city promises the benefits of a society teeming with consumer goods, while on the other it more or less blindly slaughters men caught

[1] Traffic accidents in general cause over 200,000 deaths a year. In proportion to the number of vehicles, the countries with the most deadly road traffic are: (1) Brazil (very much in the first place), (2) Germany, (3) France. Concernng violence in the modern world, see F. Hacker, *Aggression. Die Brutalisierung der modernen Welt* (Vienna, Munich and Zürich, 1971) and R. D. Laing and D. G. Cooper, *Reason and Violence* (London, 1964).

in the cogwheels of producing them. Our society, the manufacturer of "goods", is also a manufacturer of waste. No civilization has so loudly publicized the benefits of its products, yet
none has so wantonly destroyed the biological harmony of the
globe (both flora and fauna), pillaged its mineral resources (near-
exhaustion of petroleum) and cluttered up its land and sea with
litter, harmful and indestructible secondary products and anti-
values that mankind does not know how to get rid of. Raw
materials do not reproduce themselves at the speed of our manu-
facture and often enough dwindle as a result of it. For example,
the pollution of breathable air is growing from 4 to 5% a
year as a result of the outflow of energy.

Let us suggest some typical sources of the various kinds of
mortal violence rife in our civilization.

(a) Certain situations are characterized by a lack of harmony
in social interconnections, by an absence of foresight and co-
ordination (road accidents, for instance, from the point of view
of those in authority). We are referring here to a lack of rationality which ought to be corrected or diminshed as civilization
progresses. Here the Church can do no more than recall the
traditional norms, often unknown or forgotten, of the virtue of
prudence, practical wisdom, timely judgment and adaptation
to the concrete situation. In a general way it is not for the
Church to do the work of civil society but to proclaim the duty
of those in authority while taking care to carry out what it is
bound to do and what is within its reach, in the same sector
of activity (cf. Matt. 7. 1–5).

(b) In cases where violence is inherent in man (such as murder
or road accidents from the point of view of the motorist or
pedestrian), both civil society and the Church have an educative
function. In cases of inadequately controlled aggressivity, the
moralizing role of the Church comes to the fore.

(c) A third source of social violence lies in the telluric forces
that civilization has awakened but that the sorcerers' apprentice
cannot control. Nature is wild and blindly, pitilessly cruel. In
periods of calm between cataclysms, we tend to forget this because we are romantic. We rightly defy nature, but not without
risk. Progress is bought with physical and intellectual endeavour,

but is also paid for with human blood which the machine scatters and the earth grinds. Matter is no less cruel than man.

(d) Finally there is the violence inherent in the decisions of those in authority—wars, death sentences, violent repression of uprisings, police torture, negligence in the ecological sphere, etc. Individual responsibility is confused with collective responsibility, although the one should not detract from the other.[2]

The increase of gangsterism, accidents and murders stems from the individual freedom of the immediate agent and the collective organizations whose task it is to watch over everyone's safety. On the other hand, there are differences of degree between the voluntary, the accepted and the tolerated. Voluntary actions (wars, executions, etc.) usually have a positive aspect—whether real or presumed—on the side of the common good, an aspect found much more rarely in tolerated actions, apart from the necessary general freedom of the citizen. Finally, not all violent, useless and avoidable deaths are bloody. The social machine can grind coldly, silently, without apparent scandal.

Every period of history has been bloody and violent. But violence shocks us more nowadays because we hoped for deliverance owing to our technical and scientific knowledge and the progress made by mankind's moral conscience. The process of secularization has radicalized violence as much through its radicalization of rationalism, which in its aridity rebounds against the human, as through its dialectical exacerbation of the irrational which is beginning to submerge us.

2. The Necessity yet Inadequacy of a Call to Traditional Principles

Faced with the ills that beset us, the Church should join in the universal cry of pain so as to show its solidarity with mankind. Faced with man's faults, the Church should denounce sin at the same time as announcing the redemption obtained through Christ. What the Church says in its affirmation of the moral law is normative, while its word is prophetic when dealing with eschatological fulfilment. When it has the means

[2] Cf. H. Lepargneur, "Responsabilidade coletiva e pecado", *Revista Eclesiástica Brasileira* XXX, 119 (Sept. 1970), pp. 538-67.

of exercising power in the world, the Church can also seek to bring pressure to bear on the forces acting within history (political power, diplomatic activity, information, etc.), although the exercise of temporal power never escapes the contamination of sin.

The Church's moral teaching poses several serious questions today.

(a) Can the Church, having used violence so often in the past to fight or eliminate its enemies, preach perfect gentleness without hypocrisy just now when it has been deprived of most of the weapons of earthly combat? The Church's historical conscience should make it humble, but it should not prevent it from making the pronouncements that it has to make. And let us not mask evil by soothing words. Love, the true answer to evil, achieves nothing by denying it.

(b) Would not everything be solved if the Church both preached and practised radical and absolute non-violence? It is certain that non-violence has affinities with the spirit of the gospel.[3] It is necessary to point out, however, that absolute non-violence is a utopia, and that if it helps to resolve certain problems in practice it is not adapted to all or even to most of them. Moreover, violence is not synonymous with absolute evil or even with sin. The Kingdom of God itself belongs to a violent man of a certain type.

(c) Is the Church's moral teaching not utopian? In the context of the dialectics between ethics and law, the Christian faith certainly favours the side of ethical inspiration, not the side of juridical decision such as structures society. In a world without Christian faith and that is often sceptical about an eventual "natural law", there is no doubt but that gospel morality or ecclesiastical preaching is largely utopian. But as the leaven of history, and if its conscience so prompts it, the Church must speak out, even if only a few people will effectively profit from its words. It is in any case impossible to measure the spiritual

[3] Cf. H. Lepargneur, "Introdução a uma teologia da não-violência evangélica", *Revista Eclesiástica Brasileira* XXV, 4 (Dec. 1965), pp. 220–56, and "La haine est un amour déçu", *Revue de l'Université d'Ottawa* XXXII—1 (Jan. 1962), pp. 45–60.

or temporal effectiveness of true words. Our problem is first and foremost to ensure that the Church's words should be true.

(d) Have the "eternal principles" not been stated often enough? As with dogma, and perhaps more so, ethics should be formulated in words suited to the level of the people themselves and also to the time. This already offers scope for work and research, especially if we take note of the corrosive action induced by modern society regarding the true or alleged eternal principles of morality. In the matter of papal or episcopal recommendations, we would hope for a clearer distinction between "exhortatory texts" and normative texts, but there are two even more important factors. Firstly, there should be greater homogeneity between word and deed, between edifying, exoteric or moralizing discourse and diplomatic activity (often secret) or political activity (never acknowledged as such: "The Church doesn't meddle in politics"). Secondly, there should also be a greater discretion, a recognition of the positive value of silence in many situations. Too much talk dilutes the importance of words into a flow that commands less and less attention from a public submerged by contradictory messages which are often more attractive than the much-diluted ecclesiastical texts.

(e) Are Christians justified in leaping from an attitude of contempt for the world to one of an absolutization of this life? After having preached "the other world" with a certain amount of exclusivity, are we—in the name of the same gospel—going to confer on our biological life an importance that borders on the absolute? Certainly life and health are our most precious natural assets and we have what we are, body and spirit. And yet a steep upgrading of natural values runs a risk within the secularizing process of a hypertrophy that would deviate from the Christian tradition. Besides, the instrument of violence is always an instrument forged on behalf of some kind of liberation. Sometimes it passes from the project of liberation to the act of violence without changing hands.

"Don't make your car into a weapon whose first victim you could be," runs an apt propaganda slogan. How could the man who controls so badly the machinery of his own body control the natural forces which he manipulates in the name of "progress"? We cast the iron wrested from the bowels of the earth, but the steel slips through our hands. The manufactured tool is no more perfectly subject to human freedom than is nature. Its force of inertia, its underestimated potentialities, the devil inside it, seem to turn the instrument, the artificial world, the city where we live, back against its manufacturers and masters. Other considerations bring out still more the real yet relative value of biological human life. Countless heroes, wise men or founders of religions, such as Socrates and Jesus, have voluntarily "given their lives" (John 10. 18) for a great cause. It is indeed the image of the "good shepherd" (John 10. 11). The martyrs have equally given their lives for a higher good and for other causes soldiers and scientists have accepted mortal risks without being blamed for doing so.

II. In Search of a New Prophetic Vitality

The prophetic mission of the Church is carried out at the episcopal level of the diocesan Church, the regional level of the Bishops' Conferences and the universal level of the Roman Magisterium. The role of Christians in the world is also very diverse and this is the result of their individual and collective situation. (Christian groups have their specific duties according to their vocation or goal.) This, of course, includes the specific witness of priests and nuns.

1. The Exercise of the Critical Function of Denunciation

(a) *Let us not be pharisaical.* All power in this world is latent violence and, as an institution in the world, the Church possesses power which varies from place to place both in its form and in its importance. Even in a country where the Catholic Church is humiliated, it should feel solidarity with the presence of the Church in other parts of the world and with its history since Constantine (cf. Luke 6. 37–42).

(b) *Let us be evangelical.* The point is to save, not principles, but human beings (Rom. 3). The sabbath is made for man (Mark 2. 27). All application of the law should be inspired by the spirit of the gospel. Those responsible in the Church must behave as ministers of reconciliation (2 Cor. 5. 18–20). Gospel morality is not a morality of pure principles such as would give scant interest to results. Violent death is usually the result of an option that has to do with a value, and not the specific object of a perverse decision. We have not yet measured the distance that separates a morality of principles (rather blind where its fall-out is concerned) and a morality which aims at choosing the lesser evil among several evils not all of which can provenly be avoided. We should not, however, simplify things by describing the option as one that operates between an optimistic morality and a pessimistic morality. The morality of principles may take its inspiration from Jansenism and the morality that is more attentive to results may correspond to a more jovial and progressive praxis; both can accommodate the dogma of original sin.

(c) *Let us be realistic.* We must face facts without being their slave. Our faith should make us weigh them, not disregard them. Let me give four examples: (i) In the matter of abortion, if the proportion of secret abortions and the risks they entail do not impose a solution, they at least contribute to the data of the problem. (ii) Is the three-year-old child in a famine area, a child aware of the pain and death that lies ahead as a premature, unchallenged, unjust and revolting destiny, any less worthy of our attention than a foetus that is perhaps not viable or certainly deformed? (iii) There is no known example in history of socioeconomic development which does not involve a high human price in terms of every kind of victim. If this human price were to be altogether eliminated then progress would be paralysed. But stagnation, too, brings its toll in suffering and human lives. (iv) Peace as it is known in history is always an imperfect, unstable and threatened peace, a peace made up of mutual concessions, patience, tolerance, forgiveness, endurance of small injustices and also Machiavellian calculations. The politics of "all or nothing", of the perfect, runs the risk of being sterile and purely verbal.

(d) *Let us have a sense of history.* We should collaborate with all men of good will to analyse the causes of violence and its workings since our Christian principles are insufficient to bring about an immediate and effective remedy. Thus in the matter of so-called non-violent protest, let us examine the political dimensions which always exist in concrete action or the effective result may well be in danger of going counter to our good intentions.

The mission of the prophet is not to govern. If he succeeds in discussing with those responsible this does not mean that he is taking their place. It is utterly absurd to talk about capital punishment without reference to the degree of maturity among the people for whom one is speaking. Also we must not be surprised if developed nations or sections of society, which in the past have voted for the abolition of capital punishment, come to see it as opportune again today—in a specific context.

2. For a More Constructive Prophetism

(a) *The pluralism of vocations and the responsibility proper to Christians*. If we cannot reduce Christian morality to principles, still less can we reduce the Church's prophetic role to the teaching delivered by its magisterium. The Church's critical and constructive effort should be the action of all the members of the Church community. The Church should help each person to find his own vocation and to contribute as an individual to the collective development. Situations play their part in vocations. On the other hand, the Holy Spirit inspires charismas which have a concrete relationship with the needs of communities and individuals, at the moment in question. Theology should confidently state this, not so as to encourage some kind of blessed indolence but so as to kindle the sense of responsibility.

We know the general direction that the Christian should take. "The central duty of the Christian today is peacefully to put forward the claims of the oppressed, bear witness to poverty, and proclaim the demands of justice."[4] Even if we cannot say with Jacques Ellul that "if violence breaks out anywhere, the fault always devolves on Christians", the Church and Christians should never feel unconcerned or at ease when there is violence. The gospel should be a force against the inevitability of violence, the triumph of this force being less historical than eschatological. Following this line, we should ask ourselves whether the messianic role of Christians should not invite them to take on themselves—rather than unloading it on to unbelievers—the impact of a violence that nothing has yet managed to oust from our history. It is not exactly what is suggested by a map of the world,

[4] J. Ellul, *Contre les violents* (Paris, 1972), p. 191.

where the rich countries beget a primary violence which then falls into others. This is not to say that the Church should impose non-violence as a radical and universal solution. One would nevertheless like the Church not to be so opposed to charismatic non-violent vocations, for instance in the area of conscientious objection.

(b) *Pastoral or political humanization of life.* In its pastoral teaching, the Church fights sin because it pursues the values of life—of eternal life essentially, but with its secular and historical supports, counterparts, symbols and fruitions. Dedicated though it is to ultimate realities, the Church is also a community existing here and now and does not scorn the order of penultimate realities. The fight against sin, ignorance and error and for an open humanism sows the seed of diminishing violence and progressive pacification. The Church must have no illusions, however, as to its power over States, a power that is exercised through individuals, the only possible subjects of conversion. The State has no heart, but only a policy backed by an ideology. No "recipe" can be put forward as a magical solution. It is essential, however, that reflection about the new human situations should develop within the Church. It would be illusory systematically to multiply norms that are external to consciences. What is most lacking is the spirit, the sense of the human, and especially the exercise of practical reason that St Thomas called *prudence*, mistress of the moral virtues.

(c) *Prophetism and perspective.* Prophets have pride of place over casuistic moralists because, in the strength of the Spirit, they have keener hearing, sharper sight and a wider horizon. However, to each his task. Is the sharp increase in killing a matter for morality or is it to do with destiny—a sign of the times—to be interpreted eschatologically by the prophet? Whatever the answer, it is important not to confuse courage with radicality. Radicality in its forms and attitudes often expresses a flight from reality, a reluctance to elaborate one's position or adapt one's reaction to a complex situation, an abdication masked by aggressiveness. Even the option of often-courageous non-violence, if it is to be realistic, cannot remain at the simplicism of a principle. There are more radical Christians than courageous Christians, because radicalism is at ease far from danger while courage can only affirm itself within danger. Is this not one of the reasons for Christianity's lack of effectiveness in its fight against avoidable and harmful violence?

Instead of leading the common conscience of mankind, the Church often merely follows it after some delay. At a time when the most far-sighted scientists are issuing grave warnings concerning the impasse reached by our current technical progress, Catholic voices on the whole content themselves with repeating the idyllic version of reconciliation with the world embodied in *Gaudium et Spes*. And yet the Church's role is neither to make itself a mere echo of the predominant voice in the world nor to push the elaboration of a social doctrine as far as the refinement of a flamboyant utopian cathedral. In a world weary of moralistic preaching, the Church as well as Christians should avoid two extreme dangers. These are firstly that faith has nothing to do with works and secondly that faith consists of altruistic behaviour.

From the Church, the custodian of the eschatological dimension of history, we could expect a wider perspective. Christian convictions regarding the immutability of human nature has forearmed it only too well against the upheavals of particular situations and the Church is not always able to discern historical change and draw consequences from it for moral teaching. In what concerns us especially, this moral teaching should not be reduced to an assemblage of principles *a priori* nor to a methodology of attribution of responsibilities *a posteriori*: it should rather help the human city to foresee its problems of tomorrow in order to lessen them through work and formation today.

(d) *Converting destiny into history and history into the Kingdom.* We have attempted to avoid all over-simplification and in particular the Manicheism that often lies in wait for the moralist broaching the theme of violence. In the name of Christ and the Spirit, the Church has the words of eternal life, but faced with the problems of human relationships in the city of today, charity does not absolve it from technical confrontations and political options. On this level of history, it should feel solidarity with all men of good will in its task of exorcizing destiny, that is to say of slowly transforming it into history and humanizing it. At the heart of this history, where there will always be too much violence, it should cause the invisible Kingdom to be built, yet not without hope that this may manifest itself in tangible signs. In a work that expresses the wisdom garnered throughout a long career, Arnold Toynbee says that he does not see how mankind can arrive at true peace without some spiritual and religious revolution.[5] All the Churches are bound to make a contribution that may help people to cleanse their restless activities of "immoderate death", before the Son of Man delivers mankind from all death.

Translated by Barbara Wall

[5] Arnold Toynbee, *Surviving the Future* (London, 1971).

Josef Mayer-Scheu

Compassion and Death

I. Dying in Hospital

In most countries in western Europe well over half of all the dying spend the last part of their life in hospital. The large number of people dying in hospitals will continue to grow. Is it worth their trouble to live through this last phase of their life—just before death?

The answer in most cases depends on *whether* and *how* in our hospitals it is possible to help the dying compassionately in a way equivalent to the medical possibilities. An initial problem for those seeking to give humane aid to the dying is, however, that of telling sick people the truth.[1] This problem concerns not only doctors, nurses, psychotherapists and other members of the therapeutic team who are in direct contact with the patient, but a dying person's friends and relations.

There are special features to the dying and death of a man in a hospital. Since death has to be confronted as institutional enemy number one, and the number of dying patients is really enormous, medical and nursing staff have developed an especially strong self-defensive screen against the problem of truth and dying.[2] The specialization and automation of the diverse services

[1] Cf. E. Kübler-Ross, *On Death and Dying* (London, 1970); P. Sporken, *Menschlich Sterben* (Düsseldorf, 1972); H. Gödan, *Die sogennante Wahrheit am Krankenbett* (Darmstadt, 1972); E. Ansohn, *Die Wahrheit am Krankenbett* (Salzburg, 1969).

[2] Cf. E. Kübler-Ross, *op. cit.*, pp. 1 ff., 10 ff., 18 ff.; H. C. Piper, "Die Unfähigkeit zu Sterben," in *Wege zum Menschen* (1972), pp. 15 ff.

performed at the sick-bed has the result that frequently no one individual among the medical and nursing staff feels responsible for the agonizing personal questions of a dying person, since each is able to offer as an excuse the small part of the total necessary services for the patient with which he individually is concerned, which means that he has far too little time and opportunity to concern himself as intensively as would be required to the patient.

This situation means that the conversations between members of the medical and nursing staff are determined by the technical detail of the measures to be taken. These allow people without too much trouble to escape any personal confrontation with a dying person's questions. Such an attitude affects contact with the dying person's relations, who are left alone with their anxieties and whose questions are directly or indirectly suppressed. This problem is intensified by the relay-system, which is necessary in terms of hospital personnel, but means that in a major, intensive hospital care-unit in the space of twenty-four hours more than twenty different people can work on the body of a patient, yet often none of them will feel responsible for his personal questions.

Often patients in the first few days of their stay in the unit don't know the name of any of the people who have to do with them. The law would seem to emerge that the bigger the hospital unit is, the less chance there is of any personal treatment of a dying person. There are a few exceptions to this law: i.e., when a certain form of unit organization is chosen that favours a holistic and compassionate treatment of patients (for example, with specific doctors, nurses, and so on, responsible for specific rooms or patients, which of course also raises particular problems).

At any rate the present-day structure of hospitals strongly encourages a rejection of wholly personal care for the dying. Hence the understandable difficulty a hospital doctor, nurse, chaplain, therapist, relation or friend finds in sharing the truth of dying with the patient. Yet that is the decisive point of humane aid to the dying.

II. The Truth of Dying

The decisive question may be put thus: Are *you* prepared to share the truth of dying with a dying person? There are several objections:

1. From the relation: The patient won't be able to stand the truth.

2. From the doctor: You shouldn't deprive him of hope. Telling him about death is tantamount to killing him. Or: Ultimately everyone has to deal with this problem on his own.

3. From the nurse: The doctor is responsible for that, because he's responsible for treatment. Unrestricted information will surely have an unfavourable effect on treatment.

4. The doctor to the chaplain: That's a case for you. The patient doesn't know what's up with him. But the poor chap needs some comfort from you.

5. But the priest evades the issue too, feeling incompetent and insecure. He also finds communication easier with a bible or prayer-book than in a situation of powerlessness before the possible questions and silence of the patient.

6. Finally many people evade these problems with the following reasoning: I don't know anything I could say to a dying man. I haven't any experience so I can answer him or advise him.

III. Objections Examined

1. Many patients can stand the information that their position is hopeless, even when they are left with such a bald statement, and even when the informant opens his announcement with an "unfortunately", and says how sorry he is. For the problem of truth at a dying man's bedside is not a problem of a diagnostically and prognostically correct statement.

"Truth at the sickbed" is determined rather by our ability to enter into communication with the patient so that he is in a position to ask for, listen to, and mull over information about his condition and his treatment. We rightly shy away from announcing someone's impending death. Without any communication and solidarity between the dying person and his companion, usually any stated diagnosis or prognosis regarding the impending death will not be taken as truth at all. Nothing more precise is expected of the companion of a dying person than the ability to deal with one's own anxieties, in order to perceive and sustain what moves the patient most profoundly:[3] the denial of reality, fury at one's own impotence, envy of another person's possibilities in life, resignation on the one hand and hope (of survival) on the other, concern about things that haven't been seen to in life (children, a marriage partner, and so on), questions about the meaning of the past and the future.

Such confrontations require first of all an acknowledgment of one's own powerlessness. Precisely that will make the dying person's companion a partner in dialogue who really understands and co-operates. For the truth of dying consists not in the justness of a prognosis of the point of death, but in a common endurance of the circumstances of dying in so far as they are shared in openness and solidarity. The problem of truth in regard to the dying is therefore just as much a problem of truth for the companion of the dying (confronting his own fear of death and his own inability to die).

2. Certainly one should never deprive anyone of hope. But a considerable number of well-grounded investigations have shown that dying people are never without hope. Instead they stubbornly hope even when all everyday hopes are brought to nothing.[4] The phrase "hopeless case" reflects much more the position of the doctor giving treatment than that of the patient. Mere information about the condition and a prognosis of no prospects can in fact be tantamount to an announcement of death that brings about death. But the alternative is not only deception of the patient or that kind of mendacity which forbids the patient to live his emotions and voice his questions. For it leaves him alone in a state of contradiction between the hypocritical hope of the therapist and his growing anxiety in view of the continuing lack of success. A basic and intentional silence and avoidance of truth is never any help to the patient's hope.

How liberating a compassionately conveyed truth can be for a dying person is shown, for instance, in Piper's[5] report of a

---

[3] Cf. E. Kübler-Ross, *op. cit.,* pp. 34 ff., 44 ff., 72 ff., 75 ff., 99 ff., 122 ff.
[4] Thus H. C. Piper, *op. cit.,* p. 16; E. Kübler-Ross, *op. cit.,* pp. 122 ff.
[5] H. C. Piper, *op. cit.,* p. 17.

woman with cancer who was told about her condition: "What I don't need in answer to my questions is obviously well-intentioned but hypocritical consolation from the nurse.... I was spared the experience of their telling me something different in the ward to what they said outside.... They used the word 'cancer', and so did I ... I was spared the degradation of tactless consolation.... And so I retained the human dignity which is an inalienable characteristic of man. I could continue to live as a human being. The most important thing was that my relations and I escaped that sad deception.... There wasn't any barrier between us. We stayed together, which is so necessary just now, and we have come closer to one another."

This experience is so seldom met with because this process is so seldom chanced by us all—doctors, nurses, priests and relations or friends—but the reason is not that truth at the bedside would take away hope from the dying person.

Simone de Beauvoir has stressed the awful pressure of the general law of silence on the possibilities of overcoming a patient's feeling of powerlessness: "When certainty was weighing mother down and it would have done her good to have spoken her thoughts, we condemned her to silence, and forced her to suppress her fears and repress her doubt. As so often in life she felt both guilty and uncomprehended."[6]

In this connection Piper refers appositely[7] to Tolstoy's story The Death of Iván Ilyitch as a serious warning to all those who have to do with someone concerned with his dying: "Iván Ilyitch's chief torment was a lie—the lie somehow accepted by everybody, that he was only sick, but not dying, and that he needed only to be calm, and trust to the doctors, and then somehow he would come out all right.... And this lie tormented him: it tormented him that they were unwilling to acknowledge what all knew as well as he knew, but preferred to lie to him about his terrible situation, and went and made him also a party to this lie."[8]

Sporken has expressed the communication of truth to the dying person with an apt simile: truth at the bedside is like a

---

[6] Simone de Beauvoir, *Memoirs of a Dutiful Daughter* (London, 1966).

[7] H. C. Piper, *op. cit.*, p. 18.

[8] Leo Tolstoy, *The Death of Iván Ilyitch* (London, 1887), p. 62.

block that I put in the dying man's way so that he can see it clearly, yet must not see it.[9] It is usually the responsibility of his companions to see whether he learns to locate this hard reality of his life, or believes he can avoid it with eyes closed.

3. Of course, ultimately everyone has to deal with this problem alone. But in order to get to that point, everyone—at least in certain stages—needs other people who stay with him and support him when he wants to express himself and his emotions as far as possible, in order to reach that stage of maturity. For to die as a *human* being means fully to exhaust in the last phase of one's life the possibilities of one's own particular life-development.[10] Precisely in a society in which death and preparation for it has become taboo most men are helpless in this last, great confrontation of their life, which affects them all the more despairingly and all the more as divorced from reality, the less dying in all its forms (taking leave, separation, fear of loss, pain) was clear to them in their life hitherto. The increasingly anonymous and technologized world of our hospitals still contributes in no mean way to the fact that the death of many people is experienced as a wholly incomprehensible, vile fate which is forced on them. Therefore a man today needs his fellow man all the more, so that intensive experiences and confrontations in this phase of life have a partner in dialogue, and do not just slip away, or even appear—burdens and oppressions —as deception and fantasy. In being listened to, in the experience of compassionate sympathy, but also of resistance, of confrontation and—not too early and precipitately—of interpretation, for the first time[11] many dying people mature to the point of being able finally to accept their dying alone.

The right to die must be seen as corresponding to the right to live, and a right to aid in dying to correspond to the right to aid in living—right up to the most intensive form, the wholly personal accompaniment of a dying person in all his needs. The aim of that kind of aid must be to help a dying person—in so far as this corresponds to the circumstances of his life—as far as

[9] P. Sporken, *op. cit.*, pp. 56 ff.

[10] P. Sporken, *op. cit.*, pp. 26 ff., 66 ff., 80 ff.; E. Kübler-Ross, *op. cit.*, pp. 35 ff., 44 ff., 72 ff.

[11] Cf. on the following, Sporken, *op. cit.*, pp. 57–62.

possible to accept and shape the last phase of his life meaning-fully.

4. Who is responsible for this help to the dying? This problem arises particularly in the hospital. In most cases the task is tacitly shifted from one to another among those concerned, but without any argument or confrontation: between friends and relations, doctors, nurses, therapists and chaplains. Everyone has good grounds for arguing that he isn't responsible. In truth every one of these groups has advantages and disadvantages as far as this task is concerned.

(a) Relations and friends usually have the greatest degree of inner closeness to the patient, and frequently enjoy his greatest trust. But rarely do they impart an overall view and understand-ing of the course of the illness. Almost always they are without that inner distance from their own experience of the process, so that they fear the effect of their own anxiety (especially that of loss). It is seldom possible for a dying man to share his needs with them because he fears that he will be burdening them with his emotions, and perhaps even lose them in so doing. Many dying men also have strong guilt feelings towards their relations and friends because they can't care for them.

In any case friends and relations must be integrated into the process of helping the dying because otherwise they would dis-turb the often carefully built-up relationship between the patient and his trusted companion.

(b) The doctor has on the one hand the advantage of medical information about the patient's condition. He is also the main person responsible for all therapeutic measures which can de-cisively influence the process of dying. On the other hand, he often feels that he is hardly competent or equipped for this personal form of assistance to the dying. He seldom has enough time to devote himself so intensively to a patient and has to choose between the special needs of a few patients and those of the whole unit. Above all the dying of the patient faces him with the limits of his art and with his own death.

(c) Nurses and therapists usually have the advantage of being closer to the patient in his illness. They are, as it were, per-manently responsible for him in his major and minor concerns. Direct body care, remedies for pain, the possibilities of fulfilling a host of small wishes often more easily opens up trust for them than for the priest and doctor. But at the same time they experience the responsibility of the doctor as a brake on individual initiative in assistance to the dying. They feel that they aren't sufficiently trained for the process and of course have so much of their time taken up by their many tasks that for a lot of them it is difficult to opt for this kind of emphatic care for the dying. For them, too, an unintegrated fear of death is also a decisive burden. Also the dying of the patient frequently confronts them with the uselessness of their care.

(d) By reason of his calling the priest is most strongly inclined towards conversation with the patient. It is also one of his primary tasks to take part in a confrontation with the patient's life-crises and their interpretation. But these advantages are often dissolved by his ignorance of medical procedures and the world of the hospital. Finally it must not be forgotten that his office does not make him a person trusted by the patient. On the contrary: he has to wear down first of all prejudices against the Church and his office, before he even comes into question as a trusted discussion partner. If his conversations aren't superficial or sealed off by ritual, he also is confronted in the patient's dying with his own fear of death, which can release his doubt of his own faith.

IV. The Ideal Companion in Death

Is it the nurses, the therapists, the doctors, the priests, relations or friends? All these groups have advantages and disadvantages for the task. No one can fundamentally opt out. Everyone is called to co-operate with the others: with the doctor's information, the nurses' observations, the relations' hints and the priest's experiences.

By what criteria is one to decide whose should be this important task of caring for the dying man? To decide that should be primarily the patient's concern, in so far as he can directly or indirectly express his opinion. He is best able to see who among those concerned has taken up an appropriate attitude to him, who is best in a position to share his feelings, anxieties and hopes, to whom he can mention and pose important questions.

This decision should generally be respected by the other persons concerned, and the person chosen should be supported co-operatively, whether it is a nurse, a priest, a doctor, a therapist, or a friend or relation, who should then belong in the widest sense to the unit team. It is desirable that those responsible in the medical and therapeutic team should ensure that at least one appropriate person looks after a dying person in this way.

Since all of us can be accorded this task by the directly or indirectly expressed wish of a patient, we are all faced with the problem whether we are prepared to face the peculiar complex of problems associated with death, in order to enter into that requisite deeper communication with a dying person.

V. GIVING UP CERTAINTIES

Hence everyone has to surrender his certainties and a portion of his own role: the doctor and nurse their visible power over death, the priest his apparently unaffected faith. It is decisive whether we are ready to become aware of our own fear, not to deny it and to learn how to deal with it.

There is a non-verbal form of communication of fear in which, unconsciously, we give out signals of fear, helplessness and hopelessness;[12] for example, if we suddenly start to whisper in the sickroom, if we regularly enter the room only on tiptoe, if the only thing we speak about at his bedside is the patient—without drawing him into the conversation.

The defensive attitude displayed in such behaviour is not concealed from the dying person, whatever care one takes—or even because one takes such care. He senses it on another level of communication, perceives the growing hopelessness around him, and notices how people draw back from him, which increases his own fear and need.[13] Often the patient experiences such behaviour as signalling an already factual social death.

How much we are unconscious of our own fears and defensive behaviour is shown by an example often cited in the literature: Leshan describes a New York hospital where a psychologist

---

[12] M. Bowers, *Wie können wir Sterbenden beistehen?* (Mainz, 1971), p. 61.

[13] H. C. Piper, *op. cit.*, p. 17.

stood in a unit with a stop-watch. He had noted the condition of the patients in the individual cubicles and their probable life expectation and measured the time between the call signal of individual patients and the arrival of the nurses responsible for them. He found that the nurses regularly hurried to the patients who were improving, whereas they were just as sure to delay their progress towards those on the threshold of death. But when the psychologist gave the nurses the results of his investigation, they were quite astonished and defended themselves. Their behaviour was clearly an unconscious expression of their defensive attitude to death. Probably this unconscious defensive attitude was shared with all those who had to do with the dying: with doctors, priests and relations.[14]

VI. POSSIBILITIES OF SELF-EXPERIENCE

Ultimately, therefore, it is a question of *my* attitude to my own death. In a hundred years we shall all be dust—but not I. For we all know about death, but we know it for the most part *only* as something known, but not as something of which we are *fully aware*,[15] as something appertaining to *my life*, as something *I* can venture into.

Yet I can make this experience in the middle of my life. If I cross a main road carelessly and a lorry hurtles by just in front of me, I experience death for a moment as one aware of it. If I allow myself to become fully conscious of this experience, then I am deeply affected by my powerlessness, by the frustration of not being able to defend myself, by the terror of thinking that everything was almost "wiped out", from the pain that I wouldn't have been able to say goodbye.

After moments like that life looks quite different. Perhaps I get guilt feelings because I suddenly see whom I've forgotten, for whom I wanted to exist.... Probably I'm grateful after such an experience and happy still to be alive, and for a short time I forget a whole lot of worries. Then I have some hint of what dying men experience in the last part of their lives, though

[14] H. C. Piper, *op. cit.*, p. 15.
[15] J. Hofmeier, "Vom gewussten zum gelebten Tod," in *Stimmen der Zeit* (1970), 11, pp. 338 ff., 345 ff.

of course each in his own way: for the most part much more inclusively and longer in fear and trust, in doubt and hope, in courage and surrender, in resignation and bravery. It is only a hint, but whoever is willing to face such experiences has the chance of seeing his life more completely. Above all he can perceive from his own experience that dying—that is, life in its last phase—has its parallels throughout life. If we see it as the culmination of all possibilities, then we understand that the last dying of a man can be prefigured in saying goodbye, in a separation, in the loss of elementary possibilities of living. The more inclusively we regard such life situations and endure the pain of loss or parting in all its forms, the more we are able to face our own dying.

It is more possible for us to bear that threefold powerlessness which always overcomes us when accompanying a dying man: impotence in regard to telling the truth (about his unfortunate condition), the impotence to give dying and death a positive meaning for this specific patient, and impotence in the face of his desire for active euthanasia.[16]

It is precisely those feelings of impotence which constantly remove our patient readiness to share with the patient the experience of finding no loophole. Patience is, however, the decisive quality by means of which we can help a dying man to see that the last stage of his life is worth living.[17]

VII. Training of Hospital Staff

In present-day hospitals the common human task of assistance to the dying must be fully comprehended—even by a dying man's relations—if therapeutic measures are to include responsibility for the kind of help for the dying that I have just sketched.

1. If doctors, therapists, physiotherapists, chaplains and social workers are to be helped to recognize at least the signals of dying people, then their training must not exclude confrontation with the question of the meaning of phenomena such as illness, pain, suffering, loss, separation, mourning, dying and

[16] Sporken, *op. cit.*, pp. 75 ff.
[17] Sporken, *op. cit.*, pp. 63 ff., 66 ff., 69.

death. In some therapist training-schools in Federal Germany the relevant problems are treated in the framework of professional ethics or pastoral anthropology, for which the hospital chaplain—as a theologian—is responsible. Of decisive significance for this instruction is his approach to the linguistic and experiential horizon of the patient—how he encounters the dying person in the hospital.

2. Even more important than theoretical knowledge of problems is practical acquaintance with them. Not only doctors and confessors, but therapists and social workers have to have some introduction to client-centred conversational therapy.[18] Conversation analyses, role-playing, case studies under personal supervision are means of extending training which can have a beneficial effect in the long run on one's attitude and capacity in work with the sick and dying.

3. The Balint-group[19] has proved to be a classic form of further training for all these professional groups: six to ten practitioners meet under the leadership of a psychotherapist regularly over a long period, at weekly or fortnightly intervals in ninety-minute seminars. On each occasion a participant reports an encounter which he still finds difficult. The group tries to reflect the behaviour of the person in question and to help him to achieve a better understanding of his relation to the patient in question, his illness and conditions, and finally to himself. My own observation shows that Balint-groups have the most lasting effect on the self-understanding of the chaplain in assistance to the dying, and on his growing ability to co-operate in and integrate with the therapeutic framework of the hospital organization.

4. On the inspiration of the pastoral movement in the USA, and above all in the Netherlands (but in its first phases also in Federal Germany,) there has developed in Europe a form of clinical pastoral education which combines the foregoing elements with others to form a training offered in courses lasting

[18] Cf. C. R. Rogers, *Counseling and Psychotherapy* (Boston, 1942); *Client-centred Therapy* (Boston, 1951); H. Faber, E. van der Schoot, *Praktikum des seelsorgerlichen Gesprächs* (Göttingen, [3]1971).
[19] Cf. M. Balint, *Der Arzt, sein Patient und die Krankheit* (Stuttgart. [3]1963).

a fortnight, six weeks and three months.[20] An important aspect of these courses is that the foreground element is not the communication of knowledge but the transformation of attitudes.

VIII. The Churches

The compassionate human contribution to the care of the dying is not only a task for every individual who has to do with the dying, or one only for those responsible for organization and therapy in hospitals, but for the Churches—especially in the provision of pastoral service to the dying in hospitals and its relation to other therapies.

1. *Integrated Pastoral Care in Hospitals.* Precisely because of the specialization of medical personnel and the growing number of dying men in hospitals, there is a qualitative as well as quantitative rise in the need for qualified helpers for the dying who are also capable of representng the aspects of help for the dying in a therapeutic team. Since the proclamation of dying, death and resurrection as a salvific event in man is one of the central tasks of the Church, the Church must before all else look into the provision of a humane and compassionate form of help for the dying, into which its task of proclamation in the hospital must also be integrated.

2. In addition to a qualitative fulfilment of this task in the form of an integrated pastoral care service in hospitals,[21] instead of a mere sacramental provision for individual patients and an appropriate training of hospital chaplains,[22] the Church must also satisfy quantitatively the requirements for assistance for the dying in hospitals. So long as the present inadequate provision of chaplains persists, we cannot refuse to acknowledge that qualified laymen must share these duties with hospital

[20] For a highly competent survey, cf. W. Becker, "Klinische Seelsorgeausbildung/Clinical Pastoral Education," in *Schriften der evangelischen Akademie in Hessen und Nassau* (Frankfurt, 1972); W. Zijlstra, *Klinisch pastorale vorming* (Asse, 1969).

[21] Cf. J. Mayer-Scheu/Artur Reiner, "Krankenhausseelsorge und ihr Verhältnis zum Pflegebereich", in M. Pinding, *Krankenpflege in unserer Gesellschaft* (Stuttgart, 1972), pp. 128 ff.

[22] J. Hofmeier, "Menschlich sterben, Postulate an die Kirche," in *Diakonia* 3 (1972), pp. 307 ff., 310.

chaplains. Perhaps a special post might be established. The training for such work would have to be similar to that previously offered to hospital chaplains. There would be a strong emphasis on client-centred therapy and pastoral-theological capacity in a social work course.

In any case, the lay theologian or assistant of the sick in the service of the Church should be allowed, in addition to preaching and distribution of communion, the right to anoint the sick, for the dispensing of the sacraments in a hospital should be integrated into an appropriate personal service to the sick and dying. Obviously the method of anointing must be appropriate to a sign of salvation and not a sign of direct announcement of death, or a magic plea for a cure.[23]

3. Pastoral helpers of the dying, like any other therapists of the dying, have to be trained in the basic attitude which alone makes the service of the dying a humane and compassionate form of assistance. They have to learn how to be companions.

A companion is not primarily a clever adviser, a well-informed expert, or a man with answers to all questions, but primarily a patient stayer and listener—a court where complaints are never rejected, but are received with understanding and sympathy. Often it is only with such help that the necessary labour of a dying man can develop: in protest against the boundaries as they close in, in expression of longing for what is lost, in fear that perhaps there won't be anything left in the end, in envy of the healthy, in bickering, in a fitful hope which is not put out, and in a gradual acknowledgment of reality. The real companion helps the dying man to experience his *own* strength, in the uniqueness of his death in which—with the help of the companion—he remains the subject of the last phase of his life and does not become the object of medical attempts to prolong life or of an a-personal religious magic.

Whoever becomes a true companion of a dying man himself becomes a sign which makes possible what may be a decisive experience of transcendence for the dying man. In such encounters a dying individual can experience that dimension of

---

[23] Cf. J. Mayer-Scheu/A. Reiner, *Heilzeichen für Kranke* (Kevelaer, 1972).

life which in the Old and New Testaments is described as the experience of God accompanying man. Here is the theological dimension of help for the dying and, in principle, of any human communciaton in moments of crisis.

Translated by John Maxwell

Alois Müller

Care of the Dying as a
Task of the Church

J. MAYER-SCHEU's article shows the central importance of the care of the sick and the dying as a Christian ministry. He also rightly limits the function of those who bear official responsibility for this in the Church. The "priest" performs only one side of this ministry, while other tasks are carried out by relatives and friends, the nursing staff and doctors.

But this does not exhaust the problem of the ministry to the dying as a task of the Church and the local Christian community. In this article, I want to look at it as a problem of practical theology. I shall not make immediately relevant suggestions, but rather indicate the theoretical and practical problems which must be seen and tackled. These problems or tasks correspond to the three basic functions of the Church, preaching, liturgy and service.

I. "Care of the Dying" through Preaching

The various contributions in this issue are in themselves an indication of the importance for the living of their attitude to death. They show how it is necessary to enable them to make their journey towards death, and how serious in all cases are the effects of repressing the idea of death. Obviously the source of the repression is mainly the irremovable terror of the event itself, not just a person's attitude to it, although the attitude makes a great deal of difference.

But what should the Church's preaching do for the attitude

to death? Has it perhaps some responsibility for the repression which has been mentioned?

1. Clergy may of course join in the general trend of repression and think up cunning ways of leaving death even out of All Souls' Day sermons, but that is not the main problem. The question is, does the inherited picture of death as a great accounting create additional fear which encourages the repression? Preaching must not let the great subject of meeting God face to face, and the seriousness of this in view of man's sinfulness, degenerate into a merciless inspection of accounts. Christians must be freed from the *Dies Irae* complex: "Then will be brought out the book in which is written the complete record ... What can I then plead?" This produces a tension which leads to the heartlessness of "When the accursed have been silenced and sentenced to the acrid flames, call *me* along with the blessed."

A proper preaching of the idea of judgment on Christians ought to follow the approach of Rom. 8. 31–9: "Who shall bring any charge against God's elect? It is God who justified; who is to condemn? It is Christ Jesus, who died, yes, who was raised from the dead, who is at the right hand of God, who indeed intercedes for us ..." (33–4). The seriousness of the judgment is revealed on the cross, which shows us the seriousness of every decision for or against God. The accounting model is totally misconceived because it remains external, that is, it ignores the deepest attitude of the person to be judged and the "prejudice" of the divine judge. "He who believes in him is not condemned" (Jn. 3. 18). The "last thing" for a human being in a sense more important than the chronological is the redemptive role of Jesus, and this gives its ultimate proof at the moment of death. In *this* sense it would be baroque to say or preach, with Bach, "Come, sweet death!"

2. The other articles in this issue have already stressed that the right attitude to death is also the right attitude to life. It means recognizing that our life is a gift, which is at no moment simply in our possession, that because of its biological and historical— in other words, finite—constitution "letting go" of it belongs as much to its essence as clinging to it, that the highest values can only be attained in a permanent dialectic of clinging and letting go. It follows from this last point that there can be no

correct timing for death, no right or wrong moment. The intensive realization of the whole, the transcendental dimension, the joyful seriousness of life can be contained in every moment, every action and experience, every decision of life—and in death. "In the midst of life we are in death" acquires a new meaning (which was perhaps already intended in the old), and this should produce a situation in which the game of lies in the face of death is pointless for the Christian. It should no longer be embarrassing or dangerous for Christians to talk about their own deaths, not in principle and not when death is close.

II. Liturgical Care of the Dying

It is right to take away from the sacrament of anointing the stigma that it is no more than a sacrament of the dying. But for the sake of the dying the concept of a sacrament of the dying has a place. It is right that death should have a liturgical and sacramental expression, since it is one of the basic events of life and salvation. All this, of course, refers to the whole liturgy for the dying, which only in particular circumstances begins with the anointing, but certainly goes on to include the sacrament of penance and viaticum and ends, as life ends, in the other rites.

1. The sacraments of the dying may be affected by the "sacramentalist" misunderstanding and be regarded as a preparation of the soul for entry into heaven analogous to the preservation of the body from decay by embalming, and with similar hurry. Where the sacraments of the dying do not concentrate on the anointing at the last moment, but are understood in the way just mentioned, a correct pastoral approach is bound to make this misunderstanding disappear. The liturgy of the dying will then be able to develop its double dimension, ritual and ecclesial.

2. The ecumenical discussions of "faith and order" should have given us the necessary caution against a reified understanding of the sacraments. All the same, taking "faith" and "word" seriously does not have to mean a lack of interest in the substance of the rite. It is not to the discredit of the believer that the performance of rituals helps him to be sure in his faith and to be happy. There is no need—except in a transcendental sense—to

labour the incarnation. It is enough to point out that embodied human beings must be taken seriously in the bodily dimension of their understanding, expression and existence.

No one, not even the modern Western heirs of the Enlightenment, can live without rituals. The liturgical rites for the dying do not have to be sacrificed to any ideology.

3. The rites have in addition an ecclesial significance. They assure all those involved of the reality of the whole Church. This is important in the care of the dying if the community of the Church has any meaning at all. Faith lives on communication, and in particular on the community of the Church, the communion of saints. The dying person's faith must be assured of the presence of this strengthening reality.

This presence must not be limited to beautiful words, which perhaps secretly draw on magical attitudes. There must be an effort to give the rites for the dying a basis in the life of the community. When the dying person has had experience of this in his life, he will have no difficulty in making the connection between it and the liturgy of the dying. The appropriate arrangements will need to be made in the local church as well as in hospitals and old people's homes. There must be attempts to form communities round the dying. The practical difficulties obviously exist, but ways must be found. Are there friends or relatives present who can be brought to realize that they too have an ecclesial role in this situation? Is it possible to form a sympathetic death-bed community in old people's homes, which would have the additional value of being a sort of training for the others? Is the same sort of thing possible in hospitals? If the staff are too busy, what about patients who are getting better? Finally in parishes, what about something like a Bona Mors confraternity with a totally new attitude? This certainly does not mean professional layers-out and wailing women, but once it is realized that continued human fellowship is a vital part of the care of the dying, some sort of liturgically and humanly discreet community action can be organized. If organized with the right feeling, it may prove to be a valuable contemporary form of community life. A community ought to be able to manage to improve on the current sociological models.

III. DEATH AND SERVICE

"Service" here stands for the activity of the Church which is directed at each and every form of human distress. It is not primarily something specifically Christian, but an implication of the Christian faith. In practice it is distinct from the "religious" ministries of word and sacrament, and is concerned with any sort of need.

In this connection, as in the whole area of service, we come up against the problem of whether the Church should try to have a monopoly of services to its members which in fact are already being performed by society or by all sorts of their fellow men. That would be obviously wrong, but it would be even worse if the Church handed over its mission of service with the bureaucratic excuse that "that is the responsibility of such and such a department". The community must see that people are cared for, and that means that it must find out where care is lacking and provide what has to be provided in the particular case. This involves many stages, from informal good neighbourliness to highly organized welfare work.

Who is there in the community whose task is to find out what unspoken worries are weighing on the incurably sick and to look for solutions? Who makes sure that relatives are not overburdened, whether with ordinary tasks or the inevitable mental strain of losing a member of the family and the necessary restructuring of relationships, or of dealing with the painful temptations of inheritance?

If our reaction is that this sort of thing would never end, and would be a hopeless task, we have to realize at least that that is what service is, and the distress is certainly real. It also perhaps brings home to us what a task is given to us as a community, and how much is left undone.

Death, in which the dying person has to give himself up, has the right to demand that the living should not be mean with their giving. This makes the Church's mission to the dying and their families itself an opportunity for learning, in life, to die for our salvation.

Translated by Francis McDonagh

PART II
BULLETINS

Giulio Girardi

Marxism and Death

THE more spiritual critics of Marxism usually see one of its
main weaknesses as a reluctance to say anything about death.
They consider this silence to be a sign of impotence in a system
whose logic asks that the problem should be passed over as
insignificant.

There are two main reasons for this silence. In the first case,
the theoretical basis of Marxism, which demands that any non-
scientific question should be treated as false or ideological, includes any problem in regard to the meaning of life, history or
death under that condemnation. The "death of man" announced
by the human sciences would remove the problem of death.

Furthermore, there is the Marxist conception of man as the
"sum of his relations", for which individual problems—including that of death—are subsumed and sublated in a totalizing
approach.

In Marxism the interpretation of death is said to be part
and parcel of the overall interpretation of the system, and primarily of the solution to two decisive questions: the relation
between science and philosophy, and the relation between the
individual and history.

In fact the theme of death in Marx's writings is much more
evident than is usually acknowledged. But it is translated into
the terms proper to another complex of problems, mainly in
connection with the two major themes of exploitation and revolution. In this sense, before saying anything about the meaning
of death, we have to analyse and contend with the actuality of

133

death. That doesn't mean that the problem of its meaning is got rid of, but that, on the basis of such an analysis, it too is posed in new terms.

Within the limits of this article I cannot possibly develop my treatment of so highly-nuanced a subject as profoundly as it deserves. I shall restrict myself to indicating what I think might be the right way to start thinking about the problem.

I. The Reality of Death[1]

Even though it was never treated systematically by Marx, the topic of death is to be found both in his analysis of capitalism as a system of exploitation, and in his conception of revolution.

1. Death and Exploitation

Philosophic reflection on death approaches it as an individual and natural phenomenon to which all men are subject, and as the prime location of equality between men. Marx's attitude represents a break with that position. He sees the phenomenon of death first of all as linked historically to that of capitalist exploitation, whose most acute aspect he is concerned to demonstrate. Marx does not study the "death of man" but that of the working-man. For it is not exactly true to say that all men are equal in the face of death. They are no more equal in the face of death than they are in the face of life. The worker's death is never a natural one, but always to some extent violent. Not only because of accidents at work to which he is constantly exposed, but because of the expenditure of his physical and mental health resulting from working and living conditions (diet, housing, and so on), and because of the time and energy consumed by work and lost to life. The working conditions of women and children are even more inhuman and fatal. The worker's family is subjected to the same discrimination in the

---

[1] Cf. Luciano Parinetto, "Morte e Utopia", in *Utopia* (June 1973), pp. 3-12. Throughout *Capital* Marx refers to the theme of death from this viewpoint; in, for instance, Book 1, ch. 10, vii (the struggle for the normal working day); ch. 15, iv (the factory); ch. 15, v (struggle between worker and machine); ch. 25, iv (forms of existence of relative surplus population); Book 3, ch. 3, ii (economies at the expense of the workers).

face of death: the infant mortality rate in the working classes is one indication among others of that. The situation becomes even more tragic in regard to the sub-proletariat, which is made up to a large extent of workers condemned to remain jobless because of the demands of production. The class structure of our society also determines the class structure of medicine, which looks after the lives of the owners much more effectively than those of the workers and their families.

Hence it is not only the product of work that the capitalist appropriates; it is not only the worker's freedom but his life that the capitalist takes from him. Those are the three indivisible aspects of economic alienation. The right of every man to life is subordinated, as far as the workers are concerned, to the demands of productivity, and even to those of the machine. Profit feeds like a vampire on the blood of the poor. Capitalism is not only legalized robbery, but legalized murder. This murderous nature of the system is expressed even more brutally in two limit-situations apparently independent of it, but in fact necessarily provoked by its dynamic thrust: war and famine.

But it does not appear in all its seriousness until its international dimensions are taken into account, together with the human cost of colonialism and imperialism, the crushed and decimated nations, and exterminated races.

And death is not just the end of life. It is also the deprivation of life. The capitalist system is therefore homicidal not only because it interrupts lives before their time but because it arrests the possibilities of life and creation for the very great majority of mankind; because it condemns men, nations and continents to under-development; and because it reduces their life to a slow death.

Hence violent death is not an accident in the capitalist system: it is institutionalized. For the workers it is not the exception but the rule. It is by the appropriation of the product of work, of the liberty and the life of the workers by the dominant class, that the violence in the system is defined.

2. Death and Revolution

Revolution is the just re-appropriation by the workers of their work, liberty and life. Therefore it is essentially a struggle against death. It seeks for the banishment of violent death in so far as it is engendered by institutionalized violence. It tries to obtain for all workers "time to live". It seeks at the same time to transform life and death. It wishes to make effective the equality of men in the face of death, while allowing all a natural death: to die after having lived.

That means assuming a total restructuration of medicine which puts it effectively at the service of all men. But, in general, struggle against death requires a transformation of living and working conditions and finally a change in all economic and political structures. The society in which the free development of each will be the condition for the free development of all will represent a major victory over death.[2]

II. MEANING OF DEATH

Even though Marx in his treatment of the theme of violent death throws new and valuable light on the problem of death, the topic of natural death and its meaning does not seem to concern him. His few allusions to death as the "hard victory of the species over the individual" are not especially enlightening. Must we then conclude, with many of his interpreters and disciples, that the question of the meaning of death, for reasons which I mentioned at the start, is alien to the very logic of the system?

I do not think so. Marxism is a theory of revolution, and of course essentially scientific, and so it must be in order to ensure that action accords with concrete reality; but it is also inescapably philosophic, or else it could not pass judgment on that reality and transform it in an historical perspective. Hence it cannot avoid the problem of meaning.

[2] Some authors, whether Marxists or no, go further, and predict the hypothesis of a victory over natural death: that is, of a complete human mastery of biological mechanisms—a conquest achieved through medical progress. I shall not develop this viewpoint here, for, however fruitful it may be, it is not linked to a revolutionary perspective and is not specifically Marxist. Cf. E. Morin, *La mort et l'homme dans l'histoire* (Paris, 1951); J. Metalnikov, *Immortalité et rajeunissement dans la biologie moderne* (Paris, 1924); *La lutte contre la mort* (Paris, [3]1937); R. C. W. Ettinger, *L'homme est-il immortel?* (Paris, 1964); J. Rostand, *Biologie et humanisme* (Paris, 1964).

As a theory of revolution, Marxism has to display the collective and class dimensions of the human condition, of the problems that it raises, and the solutions that it calls for. But that does not mean that it reduces man to that network of relations: in fact only the perspective of a society which poses the conditions for the free development of each man justifies revolutionary commitment. Consequently the problem of the individual, that of the meaning of his life and of his death, is inseparable from the problem of history.

That conception of death is defined by opposition to the religious understanding of death. It is implicit in the critique of religion.[3] It is apparent in several Marxists of a humanist bent,[4] but it is evident above all in the experience of those countless militants (one thinks, for example, of Che Guevara) who have approached—and approach—death without any hope other than that in a new world—one that they will never see.[5]

Against the religious conception of death, which it thinks of as part and parcel of bourgeois individualism, Marxism sets a revolutionary understanding. The phenomenon of death may be natural, but its interpretations are not, and cannot escape a class analysis.

The connection between death and religion does not arise solely from the fact that religion offers its interpretation of death, but from the fact that death, and more exactly fear of death, is at the basis of the religious interpretation of life.

[3] Cf. Marx and Engels, *On Religion* (Moscow, 1957).

[4] Ernst Bloch, *Das Prinzip Hoffnung* (Frankfurt a.M., 1959), 3 vols., esp. vol. 2, pp. 1297-1391; Adam Schaff, *Sartre oder Marx?* (Vienna, 1954), *Marxismus und das menschliche Individuum* (Vienna, 1965); Herbert Marcuse, *Eros and Civilization* (Boston & London, 1966); Leszek Kolakowski, *Der Mensch ohne Alternative* (Munich, 1960); V. Gardavsky, *God is not yet Dead* (London, 1973); Roger Garaudy, "Il a inauguré un nouveau monde d'existence", in *Lumière et Vie*, no. 112, pp. 13-32; G. Mury, "Le marxiste devant la mort," in *Supplément de la Vie spirituelle* (1966), no. 77, pp. 230-54; M. Verret, *Les marxistes et la religion* (Paris,[3] 1965); and, from a Christian viewpoint: J. Gevaert, "Problematica della morte nella riflessione marxista più recente," in *Salesianum* (1967), pp. 549-67, "L'ateismo di fronte al problema della morte e dell'immortalita," in *Ateismo contemporaneo,* vol. 3 (Turin, 1969), pp. 503-34.

[5] Cf., e.g., *Ultimes messages* (Moscow, 1946); *Lettres de fusillés* (Paris, 1946).

Hence there is a deep accord between one's realization of the class character of society, of the illusory character of the religious interpretation, and the necessity for man to recognize that he is mortal. It is not a question of resigning oneself to death but of assuming it. This attitude is one with revolutionary awareness, commitment and solidarity. It shows that the rejection of the beyond is not a form of resignation, but that it confers a new density on death as on life.

1. *Death and Revolutionary Awareness*

The perspective of another life in which the problems of this life will find their true resolution is a suasion against an objective analysis of the situation and a search for historical solutions. It becomes a screen between man and reality. A major effect is to prevent workers from realizing that they are exploited, and seeing the possibility of a new society. It conceals the qualitative difference between violent death and natural death. Hence it becomes a factor of the stability of the system.

But there is more to it than that. The doctrine of the immortality of the soul is linked with the Platonic anthropology of the distinction between soul and body. Yet that is only a transposition of the division between intellectual and manual labour into a class society.

Therefore, for the revolutionary, to assume his own death means to abandon the world of illusions and to have the courage of truth. It is to look with awareness at the contradictions of the present and the possibilities of the future. It is the victory of science over myth and ideology.

2. *Revolutionary Death and Commitment*

The prospect of another life deflects not only one's gaze but desire and action from this life. History is reduced to a prehistory. Therefore it is normal for man to resign himself to a transient suffering and oppression, and for him to forsake the search for ephemeral satisfactions. He is an exile whose homeland is heaven.

On the other hand, to live in the perspective of death is to discover the unique nature of earthly existence, and of each of its possibilities—which will not recur: it is to make the earth

one's homeland and to commit oneself to be loyal to it; it is
to rise up all the more violently against all forms of oppression
and exploitation, believing that those who cannot live this life
will live no other; it is to sense the urgency of struggle for a
society which offers all the opportunities of life to all men.

3. Death and Revolutionary Solidarity

For the man who lives a purely individual life, his death is
the end of the world, the victory of Nothingness and the Absurd.
Hence the thought of death is anguish for him, something which
he can escape only by means of entertainment or religion. Is
the "religious need" anything other than the desire to escape
this reality? In this perspective a moral life, especially a love for
others, which was not sanctioned by a reward or a punishment,
would be groundless. Such a belief in immortality hides beneath its apparent idealism a tenacious egotism, which is very
close to bourgeois individualism. The revolutionary, on the other
hand, conceives his life as a struggle to bring about a collective
endeavour. His personal death is not therefore the end of his
story, which is one with the history of the liberation of the
working classes and humanity. Class consciousness, which
changed the meaning of his life, also changes that of his death.
"Non omnis moriar." "I shall not die altogether", he will say,
thinking neither of his soul nor of his glory, but of his struggle,
which continues. That cause is great enough to act as the motive
for a total commitment and sacrifice: a gift without reward,
which expects no "recompense" other than the liberation of
mankind and the pride of having made some small contribution
to it.

This conception undoubtedly endows the death of the militant
atheist with a degree of nobility of no less an order than that
conferred on a Christian. Of course it leaves unanswered basic
questions such as those alluding to the death of men who have
not lived, the disappearance of loved ones, the need to choose
between one's own life and the lives of others, the uncertainty
of the ultimate success of the revolution and of history, the pre-
cariousness of this process which polarizes the life of several
generations, the absence of the hero on the day of victory, and
the threat of death which weighs on the human species: in

short, the gulf between desires and historical realities, however great they may be. At the heart of its struggle for freedom, mankind comes up against this prototype of all imposed fates: against, that is, death. Some Marxists (such as Bloch, Schaff, Garaudy, Mury, Kolakowski, Gardavsky) do not ignore these problems and do not underestimate their seriousness. But they think that ultimately it is more worthy of man to be fully aware of his restrictions than to surmount them by an illusory means.

Translated by John Griffiths

Peter Beisheim

Scientific Report about Tendencies in Modern Thanatology

AT present there is a growing recognition that as our technical urban society progresses, there seems to be a proportionate decline in the quality of life. Psychotherapy has been one of the principal sources of linking this decline with an underlying fear of dying and death indicating that the fear is possibly societal as well as individual. While every society has traditionally demonstrated itself capable of integrating death into life, through its myths, symbols and rituals, our society implies through its nuclear attitudes, television programming, funeral practices, sexual emphasis, worship of technology and ill-treatment of the aged that death and dying is the enigma of our age. Despite this pervasive atmosphere, the field of thanatology is growing rapidly with journals: *Omega* and the *Journal of Thanatology* and research groups: The Foundation of Thanatology (New York) and the Center for Death Education and Research (Minneapolis, Minn.) and courses are being taught on every educational level. While it may appear that there is a definite break in the taboo surrounding death, we are confronted with innumerable problems: (1) what is death?; (2) what are the criteria for determining death?; (3) who should define death? (4) is death natural or a disease to be conquered?; (5) are doctors to continue to fight for life (prolongation) or allow "death with dignity" to occur?

Through increased use and rapid development of medical technology, scientists in the bio-medical field recognize the need to redefine death and establish new criteria for determining when death has occurred. Traditionally death was defined as the cessation of spontaneous heart and lung activity. Over the past few years, "spontaneous brain activity" has been added, so that now and in the future, the trend will be to rely on brain activity as the central criteria. Arguments have been raised that the brain's importance should not exclude the doctors' use of other organ activity. In August of 1968, an ad hoc committee at Harvard Medical School composed of persons from various disciplines proposed a definition of brain death (irreversible coma) and criteria for determination.[1] The criteria consisted of: (1) unreceptivity and unresponsivity—total unawareness of applied stimuli by voice, body movement, or breathing; (2) no movement or breathing—no spontaneous muscular movement or respiration or response to pain, touch, sound or light for at least an hour of observation by physicians; (3) no reflexes—no central nervous system activity either spontaneous or elicitable; and (4) flat electroencephalogram—with proper use of equipment and supervision, there is no indication of brain activity. All these traits should be repeated at least twenty-four hours later and show no change.

While this approach appears to be the most favoured and utilized, members of the social and behavioural sciences are proposing that death occurs when there has been a loss of all human traits without hope of recovery. The criteria would be the nonrecognition of persons; inability to speak, move, eat or keep clean, and show no possibility of improvement. These functions are to be tested by constant monitoring of the neocortex of the brain by an electroencephalograph. The subjective element underlying this approach (what is meant by human?) causes it to be considered extreme by medical personnel who are searching for more precise objective guidelines to relieve them of the burden of deciding who is "alive or dead". There has been an increase in the number of voices asking for commissions composed of scientists, philosophers, theologians, laymen, journalists, etc., to meet yearly concerning dying and death and to publish the results in journals and other media in order to educate society at large of the involved issues rather than have these questions resolved through judicial decrees or legislative acts.

[1] Donald R. Cutler (ed.), *Updating Life and Death* (Boston, 1968).

Transplants have been considered the breakthrough which would signal man's conquering death, but the complexity of the body's immunization, lack of donors and the low rate of success in proportion to the astronomical output of resources has caused these specialists to be discouraged regarding the practicality of transplants. Even the use of "mechanical pumps" raises the issues of supply and demand—who should receive them, what would be the selection criteria, etc. The lack of organ donors has resulted in the call for "human generosity" or to perceive the donation as one of the ultimate acts of Christian charity; but if this does not suffice, then legislative acts will be initiated demanding societal ownership of the deceased body, thus guaranteeing organ banks the greatest number of healthy organs. The relationship of transplants to man's fear of death is suggested by the possibility of the ultimate transplant—the brain or head. The most obvious problems lie with the lack of volunteers, societal unreadiness, unknown psycho-sociological factors or that ability does not compel oughtness.[2]

Another method rapidly becoming contemporary technology's attack on death is cryonics—the freezing and thawing of the body.[3] The process assumes that immediately after death, while the cells of the body are still viable, the fluids will be replaced by an anti-freeze solution and the body placed in liquid nitrogen to preserve the body until that unspecified future moment when a cure has been found for the particular disease. The body will then be thawed and the individual, depending on the length of time frozen, will be rehabilitated and once again assume a place in society. The legal, psycho-sociological population and ecological problems, while almost totally overwhelming, do not seem to dissuade individuals who see this as an opportunity to cheat death and to actualize immortality. Doctors engaged in cryo-technology view the rapidly growing "cryo-cryptoriums" as a money-making scheme capitalizing on a societal or individual fear of death. The still unknowns in the techniques coupled with the fundamental fact that not all

---

[2] Alan Harrington, *The Immortalist* (New York, 1969); Alvin Toffler, *Future Shock* (New York, 1970).

[3] David Handin, *Death as a Fact of Life* (New York, 1973).

organs or tissues of the body can be frozen at the same rate of speed or temperature support their objections.

Besides cryonics, transplants and machines, there has been speculation about the use of chemo-therapy (drugs) to arrest the ageing process. By controlling this process, many bio-medical specialists feel man will be able to conquer "natural death". The problems raised by this research, like the others, are formidable regarding the consequences; but the primary question is the effect on the evolutionary process if man interferes with the "natural process of ageing". The underlying attitude of the various developments appears to be one that implies dying and death are affronts to man's dignity, control and creativity. The research-orientated physicians attempt to develop future treatments, but they appear as only means to prolonging life—a factor which does not necessarily effect a proportionate increase in the quality of life. The distinction between "existence" (prolongation of life) and "living" (total awareness and participation) appears to be the point of departure for the methods regarding dying and death.

Because the efforts or research-orientation seem devoid of "human" dimensions, social and behavioural scientists have attempted to help the individual to cope with dying and death by integrating it into their lives. Despite the denial and repression of death by physical isolation of the seriously-ill and terminally-ill, doctors have discovered that man can and does come to the acceptance of his dying and death. This acceptance has been understood generally, as positive and real rather than a passive resignation or fatalism to something beyond one's control.

Dr. Elisabeth Kübler-Ross,[4] utilizing interviews with dying patients (patients teaching how to die), has determined that they undergo a process development encompassing five stages (not easily dichotomized); (1) denial—"No, it can't be!", which acts as a buffer allowing the individual time to adjust; (2) anger—"Why me? Why not him?", which is not to be taken as a personal accusation, but usually is; (3) bargaining—"If I

[4] Elisabeth Kübler-Ross, *On Death and Dying* (New York, 1969); Avery D. Weisman, *On Dying and Denying* (New York, 1972).

do this, will ... ?"—this does not usually last long and could be viewed as the last major thrust of denial; (4) depression: an inward silence and mourning over the loss of others and self usually needing the presence of others, but not necessarily verbal contact; and (5) acceptance: the final coming to terms with the reality and experienced by the individual as a rebirth, a freedom from the fear of dying and death. Researchers have discovered that the family and loved ones also undergo these five stages regarding "anticipatory grief" which allow them to accept the death more easily. The most apparent exception is the parents and family of a dying child—their acceptance is usually achieved some time after the child's death.

It appears that those individuals who have reached the stage of acceptance have done so because they have achieved a conscious and free realization that the act of dying is a human event. The greatest pain in dying is not necessarily physical but psychic or spiritual—the pain of loneliness, isolation or rejection which may account for the heavy sedations in order to suppress this dehumanization. The reaching of acceptance can be seen as a dynamic relationship between the "individual in process" and an environment both institutional and human (family, staff, etc.). Both of these elements have been studied and have initiated concrete changes in society.

If the individual has not consciously searched for meaning in life prior to the awareness of impending death, the individual may be placed in a position of constructing some meaning from past experiences which may be an illusion, since there is nothing else. The search for meaning raises one of the many paradoxes of life—one who lives life to the fullest accepts death more easily, and one who doesn't fears it the most. Fullness of life does not necessarily mean number of experiences or chronological life-span, but rather achieving an intensity of unity/oneness through love and selfless concern for others.

The experience of "oneness" with others is accompanied by and may even be based on a sense of unity—an intimate relationship of all that is created. This "cosmic integration of creation" has been uncovered not only through interviews with dying patients, but also through highly controversial (at least in U.S.) experiments with LSD and terminal patients.[5] Only recently has the public become aware of the use of psychedelic drugs as a therapeutic tool to help patients achieve a "transcendental level of awareness", to better deal with their pain and impending death. Many of the patients without coaxing or suggesting from the therapists would undergo an experience of "dying and rebirth" leading to a more calm and integrated life persisting long after the LSD treatment. Instead of death being viewed as the ultimate end of everything leading to nothingness, it is seen as a transition into a different type of existence (destruction-rebirth-cosmic-unity). The patients experience themselves as part of this unity so that the idea of possible continuity of consciousness beyond physical death becomes much more plausible than existence ending in nothingness. Doctors, however, are still unsure as to whether these are valid insights into the nature or reality or merely delusions to avoid the pain of dying. LSD as a therapeutic tool, however, in the face of strong bias will probably not become a common practice in hospitals.

The importance of the environmental conditions necessary to allow the individual the fullest opportunity to achieve acceptance has resulted in the realization of the "hospice"—a refuge from the fear of pain (disintegration of one's life). The first such institution, St. Christopher's Hospice, was initiated by Dr. Cicely Saunders in London, England. Most of the people admitted remain on the average of two or three weeks before dying. The staff is not primarily concerned with prolonging the act of dying, thus there are no "life-saving machines" or procedural drills in heroic measures to maintain existence. The guiding philosophy is to keep the patient as consciously aware as possible, not sedated, which is achieved through minimal measured dosage of pain killers to fit the patient's needs. The hospital relies on the use of alcohol, both medicinally and socially, to cope with pain, and upon heroin (again as controversial as LSD) and/or morphine blended with cocaine in an alcohol base called "Brompton Mixture" (first employed at London's Brompton Hospital). There are few private rooms

[5] Sidney Cohen, M.D., "LSD and the Anguish of Dying", *Harpers'*, 231 (September 1965), pp. 69–72, 77–8; Jerry Avorn, "Beyond Dying", *Harpers'*, 246 (March 1973), pp. 56–64.

because everyone should be aware that dying is not to be endured without company. Instead of the use of techniques such as intravenous to nourish the body, fellow patients as well as family and staff share the task of spoon-feeding the person. Friendships are encouraged, even though the occurrence of death is daily and the pain of grief is intense. Consistent with this philosophy is the practice of not curtaining off the patient in the last few moments of impending death, but left open for all to participate as each sees fit (presence, touch, verbal) and after the death, the rest are told by either the staff or fellow patients. A far cry from the practice of hiding death by curtains, closed doors, sealed corridors and hushed whispers which is the practice of most institutions.

Through an outpatient programme, with visits by staff members, many of the patients are dying at home with the conscious support of the family. This hopefully will spread through other hospices being planned in England and United States. Ironically, the programme, which is seen as progress in caring for the dying, was once the prerogative of the family—grandparents teaching the younger generations how to live and how to die. The emphasis upon youth, mobility and pleasure in contemporary society will continue for some time into the future to isolate the aged, infirm and terminally ill.

A movement allied with the "Hospice Philosophy" has prompted the American Euthanasia Society ("Right to Die with Dignity") to promote the use of the "living will" which asks that the person be allowed to die and not be kept alive by artificial or heroic measures and that drugs be mercifully administered for terminal suffering even if they hasten the moment of death. Even though the document is not legally binding, a growing number of patient-orientated doctors, hospitals and jurists are arguing for the patient's right to make his own decision, and are responding to it as a moral obligation. This is not to be understood as advocating active euthanasia ("mercy-killing") which so far has been resisted legislatively in most countries. The "right to die with dignity" is a problem caused more by the success, rather than the failure, of new research-orientated medicine.

The growth of thanatology indicates a continual presence of the over-specialization and fragmented view of life and reality possessed by technological man. The need for total integration of life traditionally was the function of religious institutions and may once again be its role. In this regard, there is the need for theological contribution—a contribution, however, respectful of the conclusions arrived at by the other disciplines. Therefore, we await the development of a contemporary theology of death.

Biographical Notes

GARRETT BARDEN is at present teaching in the Department of Philosophy, University College, Cork, Ireland. Formerly taught in the Milltown Institute of Theology and Philosophy, Dublin, Ireland. In 1970, he did research among the Ngatatjara of central Australia. Recent articles: "The Speaking of Sacrament", *Irish Theological Quarterly*, XL (1973); "Reflections of Time", *The Human Context* (London, 1973).

PETER H. BEISHEIM was born in Boston, Massachusetts, in 1941 and is presently completing his doctoral studies in theology at Fordham University in Bronx, New York. Since 1968, he has been assistant professor of religious studies at Stonehill College, North Easton, Massachusetts, and was elected chairman of New England Region of the College Theology Society in 1972. He was invited in 1973 to be on the editorial boards of *Thanatology Abstracts* and *Thanatology Review* and the advisory board of the Foundation of Thanatology in New York. Besides contributing many positions papers to symposia sponsored by the Foundation, he has contributed "Death and Dying: Life and Living" to *That They May Live*, George Devine (ed.) (New York, 1971).

KARL-HEINZ BLOCHING was born in 1932 and has worked as a librarian, a publicist in Church matters and in adult and theological education. He is at present engaged in adult education in the department of pastoral work of the Church in Münster. He has published essays on modern literature and three books: *Der literarische "renouveau catholique" Frankreichs* (Bonn, 1964); *Texte moderner Autoren zur Meditation* (Düsseldorf, 1973); *Tod (Projekte theologischer Erwachsenenbildung)* (Mainz, 1973).

LUCIANO CAGLIOTI was born in Rome in November 1933. Graduated in chemistry at the University of Rome and has spent three years as a postgraduate at the Department of Organic Chemistry of Politecnico at Zurigo and afterwards at the Department of Chemistry at Milan Politecnico. He is now professor in organic chemistry at the University of Rome. His special interests are in the chemistry of natural substances, with particular reference to biologically active substances and biochemistry. He has published some seventy articles in international reviews.

GIULIO GIRARDI was born in Cairo in 1926 and has been a Salesian since 1942. He studied philosophy at the Salesian University of Turin (1945–49) and has a doctorate in philosophy (Turin, 1950). He studied theology at the Gregorian University in Rome (1951–53) and at the Salesian University of Turin (1953–55). He was ordained priest at Turin in 1955. He taught philosophy (ontology) from 1948 to 1969 in the Faculty of Philosophy of the Salesian University. Since 1969, he has been at the Institut Catholique in Paris, where he teaches philosophical anthropology and the Marxist criticism of religion. He is also an associate professor at the International Catechetical and Pastoral Institute, Lumen Vitae, at Brussels, which is affiliated to the Catholic University of Louvain. His publications include *Marxism and Christianity* (London, 1969); *Dialogue et révolution* (Paris, 1969); *Amour chrétien et violence révolutionnaire* (Paris, 1970); *Christianisme, libération humaine, lutte des classes* (Paris, 1972).

G BERT GRESHAKE was born in October 1933 in Recklingshausen, West Germany and was ordained priest in 1960. He studied in Münster, Rome and Tübingen, becoming a licentiate in philosophy in 1957 and doctor of theology in 1969. Since 1972 he has been teaching dogmatic theology and the history of dogma at Tübingen. He has published, among other works, *Historie wird Geschichte. Bedeutung und Sinn der Unterscheidung von Historie und Geschichte in der Theologie Rudolf Bultmanns* (Essen, 1962); *Auferstehung der Toten. Ein Beitrag zur gegenwärtigen theologischen Diskussion über die Zukunft der Geschichte* (Essen, 1969); with others, *Zum Thema: Busse und Bussfeier* (Stuttgart, 1971); *Gnade als konkrete Freiheit. Eine Untersuchung zur Gnadenlehre des Pelagius* (Mainz, 1972).

JOHANN HOFMEIER was born 15 June 1925 in Stammham neer Ingolstadt, West Germany. Studied philosophy and theology at Regensburg and spent a year as a student in the U.S.A. He was ordained priest in 1954 and spent four years as an assistant priest. After studying in Munich, he gained his doctorate in theology in 1961 and qualified to teach theology at the University of Würzburg in 1966 and is now professor in the doctrine and educational theory of religion in the department of education at the University of Regensburg. Apart from many articles in journals, he has written *Die Trinitätslehre des Hugo von St. Victor* (Munich, 1962); *Seelsorge und Seelsorger. Eine Untersuchung zur Pastoraltheologie Johann Michael Sailers* (Regensburg, 1967); *Grundriss des christlichen Glaubens* (Regensburg, 1968); *Werk unserer Erlösung. Predigtreihe über die Feier der Eucharistie* (Regensburg, 1970); *Gottes Wort an seine Gemeinde. Exegetisch-homiletische Arbeitshilfen und ausgeführte Predigten zu allen Sonntagen des Lukasjahres* (Regensburg, 1973).

CHRISTOPH KÄUFER was born in 1935 in Mönchen-Gladbach and studied medicine in Munich and Bonn, graduating in 1961. Further training in the U.S.A., finally qualifying in 1963 and practising pathology from 1963 to 1965. From 1965 at the University Clinic in Bonn (surgery), with permission to lecture (1969) and rank as professor (1973) and leading clinician, specializing in cerebral death and general surgery.

ELISABETH KÜBLER-ROSS was born in Zürich in 1926. Studied at the University of Zürich. M.D. 1957. Present position: International Consultant in the Care of Dying Patients and their Families, Psychiatrist, Author, lecturer. Previous positions: Medical Director, Family Service and Mental Health Centre of South Cook County, Chicago Heights, Illinois; International Consultant in the Care of Dying Patients and their Families, 1970–73; Assistant Professor of Psychiatry, University of Chicago, 1965–70; Chief of Consultation and Liaison Section, La Rabida Children's Hospital and Research Centre, University of Chicago, 1969–1970; Assistant Director, Psychiatric Consultation and Liaison Service, University of Chicago, 1957–1969; Associate Chief, Psychiatric In-Patient Service, University of Chicago Hospitals, 1966–7; Acting Chief, Psychiatric In-patient Service, University of Chicago Hospitals, 1966; Instructor in Psychiatry, Colorado General Hospital, University of Colorado School of Medicine, Denver, Colorado, 1963–5; Fellow in Psychiatry, Psychopathic Hospital, University of Colorado School of Medicine, 1962–3.

HUBERT LEPARGNEUR was born in Paris 13 May 1925 and is a Dominican. He has been teaching theology in Brazil since 1958 and is at present at the Senior Seminary of São Paulo. Among his most recent publications are *A secularização* (S. Paulo, 1971); *Liberdade e Diálogo em Educação* (Petrópolis, 1971); *Introdução aos Estruturalismo* (S. Paulo, 1972); *Esperança e Escatologia* (S. Paulo, 1974).

JOSEF MAYER-SCHEU, born 12 April 1936 at Mainz, is an Oratorian working in Heidelberg, where he qualified as a lawyer and completed his theological studies in 1961. He was ordained priest in 1969 and is at present an assistant priest at the various University clinics in Heidelberg, where he also works in a training centre for clinical pastoral care. He has published, among other works, with A. Reiner, *Heilszeichen für Kranke. Krankensalbung heute,* and has collaborated in a dictionary of pastoral theology.

ALOIS MÜLLER, who was born in Basle on 20 September 1924, is a priest in the diocese of Basle and has, since 1964, been professor of pastoral theology at the University of Freiburg. Since his ordination in 1964, he obtained his doctorate in dogmatic and patristic theology. He has also worked as a catechist and in pastoral care in Solothurn and from 1959 to 1962 he taught pastoral theology in the seminar at Solothurn. He has published *Ecclesia Maria. Die Einheit Marias und der Kirche* (2nd edn., 1955); *Obedience in the Church* (London and New York 1966), *The New Church and Our Children* (London and New York 1969); *Kirchenreform heute* (1968); *Hierarchie oder Volkssouveränität?* (1970).

JACQUES-MARIE POHIER, who is a Dominican, was born on 23 August 1926 at Étrépagny (France) and was ordained priest in 1954. He studied at the Sorbonne and le Saulchoir as well as at the University of Montreal (Canada). A licentiate in philosophy and theology and a doctor of philosophy, he is at present vice-rector at le Saulchoir and a professor there. His publications include *Psychologie et Théologie* (Paris, 1967) and *Au nom du Père. Recherches théologiques et psychanalytiques* (Paris, 1972).